THE POCKET GUIDE TO
ENGLISH LANGUAGE

JOHN O'CONNOR

General editor Joan Ward

CAMBRIDGE
UNIVERSITY PRESS

CAMBRIDGE UNIVERSITY PRESS
Cambridge, New York, Melbourne, Madrid, Cape Town, Singapore, São Paulo

Cambridge University Press
The Edinburgh Building, Cambridge CB2 2RU, UK

www.cambridge.org
Information on this title: www.cambridge.org/9780521529914

© Cambridge University Press 2003

First published 2003
Reprinted 2005, 2006

Printed in the United Kingdom at the University Press, Cambridge

A catalogue record for this publication is available from the British Library

ISBN-13 978-0-521-52991-4 paperback
ISBN-10 0-521-52991-3 paperback

Illustrations by Kate Charlesworth

The Pocket Guide to English Language

SENTENCES

What is a sentence?

What makes a clause?

What do sentences do?

WORDS

Nouns and pronouns

Adding to the noun

Other parts of the sentence

CLAUSES

PUNCTUATION

Introduction

The Pocket Guide to English Language is a reference guide to English grammar. Over two hundred grammatical terms are defined in language that non-specialists will find easy to follow. For ease of use, the entries all follow a similar pattern. Each one includes:

- a brief definition of the grammatical term
- a more detailed explanation supported by illustrative quotations (from real texts)
- notes on key points
- clear cross-references to other sections

In addition to sections on sentence structure, word structure and punctuation, the *Pocket Guide* deals with important language features such as accent and dialect, idiom and figures of speech.

People often encounter two major difficulties when consulting books about grammar. The first is that many of the terms that older language-users have grown up with (noun clause, preterite, gerund…) simply do not appear in modern grammars. This is because new schools of thought in linguistics have adopted approaches which define concepts in different ways, rendering the established terms redundant. Where possible the *Pocket Guide* acknowledges these variant approaches by pointing out the different terms adopted by 'traditional' and 'more recent' grammars.

A second difficulty arises from the fact that a particular word or phrase can be defined in a number of different ways according to the perspective we adopt. For example, the word 'difficulty' in that last sentence might be identified simply as a *noun* or *common noun*, more particularly as an *abstract noun*, or, looked at another way, a *count noun*. Equally we might say that it is the *subject* of the sentence. The *Pocket Guide* acknowledges this source of potential confusion by clear and extensive cross-referencing.

Sentences 1

> A **sentence** is a unit of language which makes sense.

That explanation sounds vague. But there is no single definition of a sentence which can apply in all contexts.

For example, it is easy to find exceptions to the following traditional definitions and 'conventions':

- *'a sentence is a complete thought in words'*
  but many sentences express a single thought but seem incomplete, making sense only in context:

and many sentences express more than one thought:

> One evening of late summer, before the nineteenth century had reached one-third of its span, a young man and woman, the latter carrying a child, were approaching the large village of Weydon-Priors, in Upper Wessex, on foot.

- *'a sentence ends in a full stop, question mark or exclamation mark'*
  but many sentences have no punctuation at all:

EXIT

PM SUFFERS DAY OF DEFEATS

- *'a sentence has to contain a finite main verb'*
  but many utterances in dialogue, complete in themselves, do not:

'To walk across the moor?'
'Yes.'

finite verbs >>> page 56

- *'a sentence cannot begin with a conjunction such as* **and** *or* **but***'
  but countless accomplished writers have done this through the ages:

But what did Scrooge care?

And when the party entered the assembly room, it consisted of only five altogether...

- However we define a sentence, it has to be **grammatical**. This means that it follows accepted rules controlling features such as word-order and word-endings.
- Some linguists use the terms **sentence fragments** or **minor sentences** to describe sentences which do not conform to the normal pattern.

minor sentences >>> pages 66–7

The clause 2

> The clause is a sentence unit which itself contains the basic elements of a complete sentence.

The basic elements of a clause all appear in the following statement, taken from the sports pages of a daily newspaper:

Eriksson made Michael Owen captain only this morning.

- *Eriksson* is the **subject** of the clause. The subject is the main topic of the clause and is often the doer of the action.

- *made* is the **verb**. Verbs express actions, happenings, feelings, processes or states of being. A clause must contain a verb.

- *Michael Owen* is the **object** of the clause. The object is the person or thing directly affected by the action of the verb.

- *captain* is the **complement**. It *completes* the information about another clause element – in this case, the object, *Michael Owen*.

- *only this morning* is the **adverbial**. Adverbials add information about the action or situation.

> A clause doesn't have to include all these elements, but any clause should contain at least a verb phrase.

- The clause *Eriksson made Michael Owen captain only this morning* is also a complete sentence.
- Each element in a clause might be a single word (e.g. *Eriksson*) or a phrase (e.g. *only this morning*).
- In the great majority of clauses containing subject, verb and object, the subject precedes the verb and the verb precedes the object:

S	V	O
The patient	shook	her head
Morgan	found	a piece of gold
I	have	a dream

I have a dream

The subject 3

> The **subject** is usually the main topic of the clause and is often the doer of the action.

Examples of the subject on this page are taken from Oscar Wilde's *The Canterville Ghost*.

The subject can be:
● a single noun:

Virginia blushed

● a noun phrase:

All his great achievements came back to him again

● a series of nouns or noun phrases:

Then came *the United States Minister* and *his wife*, then *Washington* and *the three boys*

nouns and noun phrases >>> pages 24–5

● a pronoun:

He removed his boots

pronouns >>> pages 32–5

● certain kinds of subordinate clause:

What he said will remain a secret

subordinate clauses >>> pages 64–5

- The part of the clause which is not the subject is sometimes called the **predicate**.
- In most cases, the subject is easy to identify. But look at the following examples:

It was surprising

Because there is no person or thing involved in this clause, the subject is the **impersonal pronoun** *it*.

impersonal pronouns >>> page 35

'Charge it to her, like breakages.'

This is an **imperative** sentence, which has no stated subject.

imperative mood >>> pages 78–9

'Have you ever read the old prophecy on the library window?'

In this **interrogative** sentence, the word-order disguises the fact that the subject is *you*.

interrogative mood >>> page 76

The verb

> The **verb** expresses an action, a happening, a feeling, a process or a state.

These examples are taken from Jonathan Swift's *Gulliver's Travels*:

- an action:

  The wife *minced* a bit of meat

- a happening:

  It *thundered* all the time

- a feeling:

  I chiefly *wanted* to know

- a process:

  He *considered* a while

- a state:

  I *was* the third of five sons

Verbs are often described as having different **forms**. For example, the following are different forms of the verbs *walk* and *be*:

walk, walks, walking, walked
be, being, am, is, are, was, were, been

- Verbs consisting of more than one word are usually made up of a verb element and one or two **particles**: look *up to*, sit *down*, cross *over*, get *off*, talk *down to*, get *at*, care *for*.

- Verbs taking adverb particles are sometimes called **phrasal verbs**: look *ahead*, turn *back*, run *away*, go *home*.

> Verbs can be either **transitive** or **intransitive**. A transitive verb requires an object; an intransitive verb is used without an object.

object >>> pages 16–17

In these lines from the opening chapter of JRR Tolkien's *The Hobbit*:

- **transitive verbs** (with objects underlined) include:

…they never *had* <u>any adventures</u>
He *hung* <u>his hooded cloak</u> on the nearest peg
…he *spread* <u>a piece of parchment</u>

Other transitive verbs in the opening chapter are: *hear, cross, blow, take, give, make* and *want*.

- **intransitive verbs** include:

…the tunnel *wound* on and on
…they discreetly *disappeared*
…and there they *remained* to the end of their days

Other intransitive verbs in the opening chapter are: *live, go, come, hop* and *lie*.

- Although *be* does not take an object, it is not usually classed as an intransitive verb.

- Many verbs can be either transitive or intransitive, depending on how they are used in the clause. For example:

The door *opened* onto a tube-shaped hall

(intransitive: there is no object)

He *opened* the door with a jerk

(transitive: *door* is the direct object)

The object 5

There can be two types of object in the sentence: direct and indirect.

The **direct object** is usually the person or thing directly affected by the action expressed by the verb.

For example:

	S	V	dO
	I	sipped	*my tea*
Reader,	I	married	*him*

Even verbs which are not literally 'actions' can be followed by an object:

S		V	dO	
I	can	smell	*it*	
You	never	get	*the chance*	in this job

The **indirect object** is the person for whose benefit (or to whose disadvantage) the action was carried out.

For example:

S	V	iO	dO
Derby	give	*Smith*	his papers

or:

S	V	dO	iO
She	handed	her passport	*to the official*

- An object can be:
  - a single noun:

  Will you be seeing *Corky*?

  - a noun phrase:

  Catsmeat shook *the lemon* sombrely.

  nouns and noun phrases >>> pages 24–5

  - a pronoun:

  But, dash *it*!

  pronouns >>> pages 32–5

  - certain kinds of subordinate clause:

  Jeeves said *I'd be all right*.

  subordinate clauses >>> pages 64–5

- Indirect objects do not usually occur in the sentence without a direct object.
- Direct objects can be any kind of animate being or inanimate thing; indirect objects are usually living creatures.
- A set of nouns or noun phrases counts as a single object:

S	V	dO...
I	had	*eggs, beans, fried bread, bacon and sausage*

The complement 6

The **complement** is so called because it adds to or 'completes' the meaning of another element in the clause. This element might be the subject or the object.

The **subject complement** usually follows the subject and verb:

S	V	sC
You	are	*a senator*

The verbs which are followed by a subject complement are usually parts of the verb *be*, or verbs such as *become, seem, grow, appear* and *remain*. Such verbs are called **copular verbs**, from the Latin *copulare*: to link. For example:

S	V	sC
I	grow	*old*

The **object complement** usually follows the direct object, as in these newspaper headlines:

S	V	O	oC
French	elect	Chirac	*President*
Defeat	makes	me	*angry*

- A complement can be:
  - a noun or noun phrase:

  I am *thy father's spirit*

  nouns and noun phrases >>> pages 24–5

  - an adjective or adjective phrase:

  This fellow's *wise enough to play the fool*

  adjectives >>> pages 38–9

  - a pronoun:

  Are not you *he*...?
  'THAT'S *HIM*!'

  pronouns >>> pages 32–5

  - certain kinds of subordinate clause:

  'No, that's *what Corky said.*'

  subordinate clauses >>> pages 64–5

- In some clauses containing a subject or object complement, the verb *be* is omitted:

We consider these truths self-evident

The adverbial

> An **adverbial** adds meaning to a clause by telling us, for example, when, where, why or how something happened.

For example, the following sentence contains three adverbials:

> Meanwhile, a witness, Ellen Stanton, told police she had seen Alfred Stratton … tearing at high speed away from the shop.

- *Meanwhile*
  a **time** adverbial, answering the question *When?*
  Other examples include: *then, tomorrow morning, soon, next Tuesday.*

- *at high speed*
  a **manner** adverbial, answering the question *How?*
  Other examples include: *silently, slowly, by train, in haste.*

- *away from the shop*
  a **place** adverbial, answering the question *Where?*
  Other examples include: *downstairs, behind the fridge, there, outside.*

> Adverbials which consist of just one word are called **adverbs**.
>
> **adverbs >>> pages 44–5**

Adverbials are also commonly used to:
- add a comment:

> *Frankly*, my dear, I don't give a damn.

- link clauses in meaning:

> Marry, sir, they have committed false report; *moreover*, they have spoken untruths; *secondarily*, they are slanders…

- Adverbials can be:
  - a single word:

    > 'Nephew!' returned the uncle *sternly*

  - a phrase:

    > His nephew left the room *without an angry word*

  - a clause:

    > Forgive me *if I am wrong*

- Adverbials add *extra* meaning: if they are removed, you are still left with a perfectly grammatical sentence:

  > A witness, Ellen Stanton, told police she had seen Alfred Stratton.

Types of sentence 8

> Sentences can be: **statements, questions, commands or exclamations.**

- Most sentences are **statements**. The main aim of a statement is to convey information:

  My father had a small estate in Nottinghamshire.

  In a hole in the ground there lived a hobbit.

  In Troy, there lies the scene.

- The aim of a **question** is to ask for information:

  But what is the black spot, Captain?

  Are you the spirit, sir, whose coming was foretold to me?

  Who's there?

- **Commands** instruct someone to do something:

  Burn that into your head, friend.

  And please don't cook me, kind sirs.

  Bring some pepper, Mason.

- **Exclamations** are used to express strong emotions or assertions:

  How sweet the moonlight sleeps upon this bank!

  Well, come, I take that friendly!

  And you're a lout!

The terms statement, question, command and exclamation describe the **functions** of different clauses. When referring to their **forms** we sometimes use the terms **declarative**, **interrogative**, **imperative** and **exclamative** clauses.

imperative mood >>> pages 78–9
declarative mood >>> page 76
interrogative mood >>> page 76

- There are three main types of question:
  - **yes/no questions** – requiring a simple yes or no answer:

    Ever had earwig races?

    Are you here for six days?

  - **wh- questions** – involving the words *who, what, where, why, when* and *how*:

    Where's the map?

    How did you feel – in the front line?

  - **alternative questions** – offering a choice:

    Will you sleep here, sir, or on Mr Hardy's bed?

- **Tag questions** ('tagged' on to the end of a clause) are often used in conversation:

  Excuse my sock, *won't you?*

  It – it hasn't gone through, *has it?*

- **Rhetorical questions** are ones which do not expect an answer:

  Must you sit on Osborne's bed?

Nouns and noun phrases 9

Nouns and noun phrases can be defined in more than one way
– according to:

- what role they perform
- how they behave in the sentence

The role of nouns

> Nouns are words which refer to people, places or
> things (including abstract concepts). A group of
> words which does this is called a **noun phrase**.

For example:

> I had a few *words* to say to *Master Hardy*. You never saw the
> blasted *mess* those *fellows* left the *trenches* in. *Dug-outs* smell
> like *cess-pits*; rusty *bombs*; damp *rifle grenades*...

> I exchanged *smiles* now with the happy *couple* at their *hut*
> and trudged on along the *beach* to *Mudeford*...
>
> ...every second *Friday* of the *month* my *Uncle Barney* used
> to take me to the *seaside*. Regular as *clockwork*.

How nouns behave in the sentence

A word can be identified as a noun or noun phrase if:

- its use and meaning can be influenced by words such as *the, a, some, two* or *this*. These are collectively known as **determiners**:

> In <u>these</u> *times* of ours, though concerning <u>the</u> exact *year* there is <u>no</u> *need* to be precise, <u>a</u> *boat* of dirty and disreputable *appearance*, with <u>two</u> *figures* in it, floated on <u>the</u> *Thames*...

determiners >>> pages 36–7

- it changes its form to show singular, plural and possessive:

> Even the *blindmen's dogs* appeared to know him; and ... would tug their *owners* into *doorways* and up *courts* ... But what did *Scrooge* care? It was the very *thing* he liked.

- Although noun phrases are here defined as *groups* of words which refer to people, places or things, some grammarians call any single word which does this job a noun *phrase*.
- Another way of defining a noun or noun phrase is to say that:

    a noun (or pronoun) is any word or phrase that can serve as the subject of a sentence.

subject >>> pages 12–13

Different types of noun   10

Common and proper

All nouns are either **common nouns** or **proper nouns**.

> **Common nouns** are the labels of non-specific people, places or things, such as *woman, town, week* and *ship*.
>
> **Proper nouns** are the labels given to particular people, places or things, such as *Cleopatra, Glasgow, Wednesday* and *Titanic*.
>
> **Proper nouns** which consist of more than one word (e.g. *Mary Tudor, Cambridge University Press, Martin Luther King*) are sometimes called **proper names**.

For example, look at the nouns in this extract from Thomas Hardy's *The Mayor of Casterbridge*:

Elizabeth-Jane [p] developed early into <u>womanliness</u> [com]. One <u>day</u> [com], a <u>month</u> [com] or so after receiving <u>intelligence</u> [com] of *Newson's* [p] <u>death</u> [com] off the *Bank of Newfoundland* [p], when the <u>girl</u> [com] was about eighteen, she was sitting in a willow <u>chair</u> [com] in the <u>cottage</u> [com] they still occupied…

There are other ways of grouping nouns. For example, we can think in terms of:

Concrete nouns and abstract nouns

> **Concrete nouns** refer to people and things which can be experienced in the physical world such as *banana, singer, ball, margarine, clock, lemonade, Queen Victoria* and *Birmingham*.
>
> **Abstract nouns** refer to emotions, concepts and qualities such as *happiness, velocity, deceit, fear, month* and *expectation*.

Analysing the nouns in the Hardy extract in this way, we get:

Elizabeth-Jane [con] developed early into <u>womanliness</u> [a]. One <u>day</u> [a], a <u>month</u> [a] or so after receiving <u>intelligence</u> [a] of *Newson's* [con] <u>death</u> [a] off the *Bank of Newfoundland* [con], when the *girl* [con] was about eighteen, she was sitting in a willow *chair* [con] in the *cottage* [con] they still occupied...

- Words such as *day, week* and *month* divide opinion among linguists. Some prefer to think of them as concrete nouns.
- Some nouns can be both concrete and abstract, depending on how they are used. For example, the game of *football* (a concept, therefore an abstract noun) is played with a *football* (here a physical, measurable object, therefore a concrete noun).
- Concrete nouns which refer to groups (such as *herd, flock, team, committee*) are known as **collective nouns**.

Nouns can also be grouped into:

Count nouns and non-count nouns

> **Count (or countable) nouns** refer to individual units which can be counted. For example: *table, tree, teacher, station* and *idea*.
>
> Count nouns can have a plural form: *tables, trees...*
>
> **Non-count (or mass) nouns** refer to things which normally exist only as a mass or single entity. For example: *air, music, milk, help, nonsense* and *spaghetti*.
>
> Non-count nouns do not normally have a plural form.

For example, we might analyse the Thomas Hardy extract as follows:

Elizabeth-Jane [nc] developed early into *womanliness* [nc]. One <u>day</u> [count], a <u>month</u> [count] or so after receiving *intelligence* [nc] of *Newson's* [nc] <u>death</u> [count] off the *Bank of Newfoundland* [nc], when the <u>girl</u> [count] was about eighteen, she was sitting in a willow <u>chair</u> [count] in the <u>cottage</u> [count] they still occupied...

Some nouns can be both count and non–count. For example, we might go into a shop which sells *ice cream* [nc] and buy four <u>ice creams</u> [count]. We might say that *history* [nc] is bunk; but that we have read several <u>histories</u> [count] of the Great War.

Singular and plural 11

The **singular** form of the noun is used to refer to just one person, or thing; the **plural** form is used to refer to more than one. In grammar, the idea of singular and plural is called **number**.

For example:

Far in this *den* [s] of infamous *resort* [s], there was a low-browed, beetling *shop* [s], below a pent-house *roof* [s], where *iron* [s], old rags [p], bottles [p], bones [p] … were brought.

- Most nouns in English form the plural by adding -*s* or –*es*. But there are a number of **irregular plurals**, e.g. *children, wives, women, men, mice, oxen, teeth* and *people*.
- Some nouns are the same in the singular and the plural, e.g. *sheep, deer, aircraft* and *crossroads*.
- **Invariable nouns** are ones which can be used:
  a) only in the singular, e.g. non-count nouns and odd words like *Physics* and *billiards*,
  or
  b) only in the plural, e.g. *scissors, jeans, congratulations*.
- Proper names are usually invariable, except in examples such as *There were five Johns at the party* and colloquial expressions such as *The David Beckhams of this world*.
- Some plural nouns look like singular nouns, e.g. *police, cattle, people* (though we can also talk about different *peoples*).

Nouns in apposition   12

> When two nouns or noun phrases occur next to each other, and both refer to the same thing, we say that the second is **in apposition** to the first.

For example, in the phrase *my daughter, the lawyer* the two noun phrases refer to the same person: the second noun phrase, *the lawyer*, is in apposition to the first, *my daughter*.

The same applies to Roald Dahl's

Danny, Champion of the World

Here, the noun phrase *Champion of the World* helps to define and describe the noun, *Danny*. Again, it is in apposition to the noun.

Apposition has a number of different uses:
- Sometimes the phrase in apposition will express a quality or attribute of the first phrase:

Mr Robert Zwelinzima, man about town…

In this quote from Athol Fugard, the second noun phrase, *man about town*, adds information to the first, *Mr Robert Zwelinzima*.

Athol Fugard

- At other times, the second noun phrase (in apposition) is an example of the first noun phrase, as in this from George Orwell:

> ...one can even send some worn-out and useless phrase – some 'jackboot', 'Achilles' heel', 'hotbed' ... into the dustbin where it belongs.

In this sentence, the phrase *some 'jackboot'...* is placed in apposition as an example of *some worn-out and useless phrase*.

George Orwell

In the verse

A Jug of Wine, a Loaf of Bread...

the two noun phrases *A Jug of Wine* and *a Loaf of Bread* are **in co-ordination**: there is no connection in meaning between the second noun phrase and the first – it simply follows it as part of a list.

Pronouns 13

> Pronouns are words which are used in place of
> nouns or noun phrases.

For example:

> *They* could not see a sign of *him*. *He* had vanished. *They*
> yelled twice as loud as before, but not so delightedly.
> 'Where is *it*?' *they* cried.
> 'Go back up the passage!' *some* shouted.
> 'This way!' *some* yelled. 'That way!' *others* yelled.

In that extract from *The Hobbit*, the pronouns *They*, *some* and
others all replace the noun phrase *the goblins*; while *him*, *He* and
it replace the proper name *Bilbo Baggins*.

Some of the most commonly used pronouns are: *I, we, it, us,
ours, theirs, him* and *herself*.

Three common types of pronoun

Three common types of pronoun are known as **central pronouns**. They are:

- **personal** pronouns, e.g. *I, we, she, it, them*
- **reflexive** pronouns, e.g. *myself, ourselves, itself*
- **possessive** pronouns, e.g. *mine, ours, hers, its*

Personal pronouns are the most familiar type and refer to people and things:

> '*I* feel far away from *her*,' he said. '*It's* hard to make *her* understand.'
>
> '*You* mean about the dance?'
>
> All the people like *us* are *We*
> And *everyone* else is *They*

Reflexive pronouns 'reflect back' to the earlier noun or pronoun:

> '<u>He</u> built them up *himself*.'
>
> If <u>you</u> want a job done, do it *yourself*.

Possessive pronouns show ownership:

> 'I didn't know it was *your* table,' said Alice.
>
> *My* kingdom for a horse!

Older grammars would call <u>*your*</u> *table* and <u>*My*</u> *Kingdom* **possessive adjectives**; some linguists refer to all possessive pronouns as **determiners**.

determiners >>> pages 36–7

Six more types of pronoun

Other kinds of pronoun are:

- **interrogative** pronouns, e.g. *what? which? whose?*
- **demonstrative** pronouns, e.g. I'll have *this*, I'll hold *these*
- **reciprocal** pronouns, e.g. *each other, one another*
- **indefinite** pronouns, e.g. *everyone, anybody, something*
- **impersonal** pronouns, e.g. *one, you, they*
- **relative** pronouns, e.g. *who, which, that*

Interrogative pronouns are used in questions:

'*Who* do you think's going to keep you?'

Demonstrative pronouns help to indicate the position of people or things in relation to the speaker:

'…then there's those verses, you never wrote *those* out, now did you?'

So long lives *this* and *this* gives life to thee.

Interrogative and demonstrative pronouns can also act as **determiners**.

determiners >>> pages 36–7

Reciprocal pronouns refer to two-way relationships:

> Wenger and Ferguson taunt *each other*
> We are responsible for *one another*

Indefinite pronouns express vagueness and uncertainty:

> *Someone, somewhere* wants a letter from you
> ...*something* nasty in the woodshed
> When *everyone* is *somebodee*,
> Then *no one's anybody*

Impersonal pronouns are used in statements which refer to people in general or unknown people:

> *One* doesn't like to be difficult...
> *You* can't make a silk purse out of a sow's ear
> *They* shut the road through the woods

Rather than replace a noun/noun phrase, **relative pronouns** are used to *link* a relative clause to a noun/noun phrase:

> The tree ferns *that* had luxuriated in its spray had dried around the dried-up pool
>
> The Man *Who* Fell To Earth

relative clauses >>> page 71

relative clauses >>> page 71

> There is also a very common impersonal use of the pronoun *it*, seen in expressions such as *It's a fine day* and *What time is it?*
>
> Used in this way, it is sometimes called **empty *it*** or **prop *it***.

Determiners 14

> **Determiners are a class of words which help to 'determine' the meaning of a noun or noun phrase.**

Determiners are among the commonest words in the language and include:

- **articles**, which consist of:
  - ○ the **definite** article: *the*
  - ○ the **indefinite** article: *a* or *an*
  - ○ the **zero** article (the absence of an article): in expressions such as: *by train*, *in summer*
- **demonstratives**: *this, that, these, those*

This Sporting Life

- **possessives**, e.g. *my, our, his, her, its, their*

Our Town

- **quantifiers**, e.g. *some, any, many, few, much, little, all, neither*

All My Sons

- **numerals**

- **interrogatives**, e.g. *which...? what...? whose...?*

What job with Danny Boon?

Three types of determiner

- The commonest type are called **central determiners**.
  These are the definite and indefinite article (*the*, *a/an*) and
  words which can do the same job as articles, such as *this*,
  every and *some*:

  What is *this* life, if, full of care…?
  Every little thing she does

- **Predeterminers** occur before central determiners. They are
  nearly all to do with quantity and include *all*, *both*, *half* and
  twice:

  Yea, *twice* the sum
  …but you cannot fool *all* the people *all* the time

- **Postdeterminers** occur after central determiners. They are
  to do with number and include: *one*, *two*…, *first*, *second*…,
  many, *several*, *few*, *lot of*:

  The *Seven* Pillars of Wisdom
  The *Last* Picture Show

Determiners are only classed as determiners when they
precede a noun; when they don't they are classed as
pronouns:

| And *all* shall be well | **pronoun** |
| *All* the President's Men | **determiner** |

pronouns >>> pages 32–5

Adjectives 15

> An **adjective** is a word which gives more information about, or picks out some feature of, a noun or pronoun. In some grammars it is said to **modify** the noun.

pre- and postmodifiers >>> pages 40–1

For example:

> A *good*, *honest* and *painful* sermon
>   I grant him *bloody*,
> *Luxurious, avaricious, false, deceitful…*
> I could see that, if not exactly *disgruntled*, he was far from being *gruntled*

The adjective can occur:
● immediately before the noun:

> I'm not the *heroic* type really.

Adjectives in this position are called **attributive** adjectives.

● on its own as a complement:

> You cannot be both *fashionable* and *first-rate*.

Adjectives in this position are called **predicative** adjectives and usually follow the verb *be*.

complement >>> pages 18–19

Both uses are found in Wilfred Owen's

> That is why the *true* [attr] poets must be *truthful* [pred].

Sometimes the adjective immediately follows the noun. This happens:

- in set phrases such as:

  proof *positive*, time *immemorial*

- after indefinite pronouns:

  something *unexpected*, anyone *interested*, anything *possible*

pronouns >>> pages 32–5

- in expressions which have been in the language for a long time, such as these which appear in Shakespeare:

  ...were it not here apparent that thou art *heir <u>apparent</u>*
  ...the *crown <u>imperial</u>*

- Attributive adjective *phrases* often go after, rather than before, the noun:

  The Diamond *as Big as the Ritz*

- The same word can be a noun or an adjective depending on its use:

  The short and simple annals of the *poor* [n]
  The *poor* [adj] man at his gate

Modifiers 16

> Modifiers help to make the meaning of a noun phrase more specific.

Premodifiers

Words which come between the central determiner (e.g. *a/an*, *the*, *every*, *some*) and the noun are called **premodifiers**.

determiners >>> pages 36–7

● Premodifiers are usually **adjectives**:

> ...the *sloeblack, slow, black, crowblack, fishingboat-bobbing* sea

● But they can be **participles**:

> I was born under a *wandering* star
> At the still point of the *turning* world

participles >>> pages 58–61

● Or **nouns** used adjectivally:

> Dickens's A *Christmas* Carol
> Massinger's The *City* Madam
> Wycherley's The *Country* Wife

Postmodifiers

Words in the noun phrase which appear after the noun are called **postmodifiers**.

These can be:

- **prepositional phrases**:

  Tennessee Williams's Cat *on a Hot Tin Roof*
  Hardy's The Mayor *of Casterbridge*
  Shakespeare's Much Ado *About Nothing*

prepositions >>> pages 46–7

- **clauses**:

  The man *who listens to reason*
  The house *that Jack built*

clauses >>> pages 50–1

It is common to find a noun accompanied by both premodifiers and postmodifiers:

	premodifier/s	noun	postmodifier/s
The	Merry	Wives	of Windsor
the	moving	toyshop	of their heart
The	daring young	man	on the flying trapeze

Comparative and superlative

> The comparative and superlative forms of the adjective are used to express a difference.

Traditionally, the comparative expresses a difference between two things (*the younger sister*), and the superlative between more than two (*the youngest sister*).

- Some adjectives form comparatives and superlatives through the use of *-er* and *-est* endings:

  smaller / smallest
  tidier / tidiest
  louder / loudest

- Others – especially longer adjectives – use *more* and *most*:

  more / most interesting, beautiful, expensive, user-friendly

- And some are irregular:

  bad / worse / worst
  good / better / best

Shakespeare's comparatives and superlatives

- Many of Shakespeare's comparatives and superlatives follow the conventions outlined opposite, i.e. shorter words with *-er/-est*, longer words with *more/most*:

  Sir, your company is *fairer* than honest

  A little ere the *mightiest* Julius fell

  Why, saw you anything *more wonderful?*

  Most wonderful!

- However, he sometimes uses the *-er/-est* forms with longer adjectives where we today would use *more/most*:

  Nothing *certainer*

  I have learnt by the *perfectest* report

- And he occasionally employs a double comparative or superlative:

  How much *more elder* art thou than thy looks

  This was the *most unkindest* cut of all

- We even find:

  To taste of thy *most worst*

  and the apparently contradictory:

  Against the envy of *less happier* lands

Adverbs 18

> Adverbs have a wide range of uses. They can add information to a verb, an adjective, a pronoun, a noun phrase or another adverb, and they also connect clauses and sentences.

- Adverbs very commonly act as the adverbial element in a clause:

  ...tomorrow we shall die!

  I have dared to love you *wildly, passionately, devotedly, hopelessly.*

adverbials >>> pages 20–1

- Adverbs such as *very, extremely, really, nearly, remarkably, quite* and *hardly* are also widely used to add to the meaning of an adjective or another adverb:

  To die will be an *awfully* <u>big</u> [adj] adventure.

  ...to speak *quite* <u>candidly</u> [advb]

Used in this way, the adverb is sometimes called an **intensifier**.

- They can also be found with pronouns:

  Nearly <u>everyone</u> [pron] who witnessed the crash agreed that...

  And with noun phrases:

  I am not *quite* <u>a gentleman</u> [noun phr]

- Adverbs such as *however, meanwhile, moreover* and *nevertheless* can also act as **conjuncts**, linking sentences or clauses in meaning:

  ...and leave to simmer. Meanwhile prepare the vegetables...

conjuncts >>> page 49

Adverbs and adverbial phrases help to answer questions such as *When? Where?* and *How?*

- If they usually answer the question *When?* they are **time adverbials**, e.g. *today, tomorrow, now, then, soon, recently, in a minute, after lunch, for a month.*

  Today we have naming of parts.
  They sailed away *for a year and a day*

- If they usually answer the question *Where?* they are **place** (or **space**) **adverbials**, e.g. *inside, here, there, everywhere, downstairs, under the car, in school.*

  The buck stops *here.*
  I left my heart *in San Francisco*

- If they usually answer the question *How?* they are **manner** (or **process**) **adverbials**, e.g. *quickly, silently, amazingly, astronomically, by train, with a spoon.*

  I *distinctly* said 'Pineapple chunks' at the canteen.
  I heard it *through the grapevine*

Prepositions

> A **preposition** is a word which can be placed before
> a noun, noun phrase or pronoun ('pre-positioned')
> in order to create a **prepositional phrase**.

Most common prepositions are very short words which help to
express relationships, especially to do with time or place, e.g. *in,
on, at, to, for, by, with, from, under, over, round, below, above, near,
after, before, since, until, till*.

> Here we go *round* [place] the prickly pear
> *At* [time] five o'clock *in* [time] the morning.

- Prepositions usually occur before nouns, noun phrases or
  pronouns:

> ...but *for* <u>Wales</u> [noun]!
> Now I hold creation *in* <u>my foot</u> [noun phr]
> I'll dig *with* <u>it</u> [pron].

- But they can occasionally be found, for example, before
  adjectives or adverbs:

> *In* <u>brief</u> we need to act quickly [adj]
> Oh, *in* <u>there</u> [advb]. I'd say anything in there!

Simple and complex prepositions

The prepositions on page 46 are all one-word **simple prepositions**.

But there are a number of **complex prepositions**: two- or three-word phrases which function in the same way as a simple preposition. These include *according to, as well as, except for, in favour of, ahead of, apart from, near to, in spite of, because of, in addition to* and *on behalf of.*

- Some prepositions, such as *in*, can also be used figuratively:

  If you're *in a hole*, stop digging.

  or in set expressions:

  Do not fall *in love* with me
  On Wenlock Edge the wood's *in trouble*

- Many of the words listed as prepositions on page 46 can also be used as:

  ○ conjunctions:

  Wait *till* the sun shines, Nellie

  conjunctions >>> pages 48–9

  ○ adverbs:

  And Jill came tumbling *after*.

  adverbs >>> pages 44–5

  ○ adjectives:

  …while he is *near*

  adjectives >>> pages 38–9

Conjunctions 20

> Conjunctions are words which join together
> ('con-join') two or more words, phrases or clauses.

There are two kinds:
- co-ordinating conjunctions
- subordinating conjunctions

Co-ordinating conjunctions

The most common co-ordinating conjunctions are *and*, *but* and
or. They are used to join two words, phrases or clauses which
are:

a) of the same type (e.g. both nouns or both statements),
   and

b) carry the same weight (i.e. neither element is more
   important than the other).

Co-ordinating conjunctions can join:

- single words, such as nouns or adjectives:

  Jack *and* Jill went up the hill.

  safe *and* sound

- phrases:

  Add three cloves *or* an ounce of ground cloves

- clauses:

  Mr Jones of the Manor Farm had locked the hen-houses
  for the night, *but* was too drunk to remember to shut the
  pop-holes.

Subordinating conjunctions

Subordinating conjunctions help to show the connection in meaning between the main clause and the subordinate clause.

main and adverbial clauses >>> pages 63 and 72–5

Conjuncts

Conjuncts are not conjunctions but adverbials. Whereas conjunctions link elements only within the sentence, conjuncts can also show the links between sentences and paragraphs.

Conjuncts are used where the writer or speaker needs to:
- order information, e.g. *first of all, to conclude, moreover*
- show links, e.g. *for example, for instance, in other words*
- make a logical step, e.g. *therefore, as a result, consequently*
- introduce counter-arguments, e.g. *on the other hand, instead, however*
- change the subject, e.g. *by the way, incidentally*
- explain contemporaneous action, e.g. *meanwhile, in the meantime*

Conjunctions and conjuncts are sometimes collectively known as **connectives**.

Clauses

> A **clause** is a part of a sentence which itself contains
> all or some of the elements of a sentence. All the
> following examples of clauses are also complete
> sentences.

A clause has to contain at least a **verb**: any part of a sentence
without a verb cannot be a clause.

Most clauses will also have a stated subject:

> Jesus wept   [one clause: **S** + **V**]

subject >>> pages 12–13

Many will also have a direct object:

> I saw ten thousand talkers   [**S** + **V** + **dO**]

object >>> pages 16–17

Some will have all the possible elements:
subject, verb, object, complement and adverbial:

> England get their knees brown in Australia

complement >>> pages 18–19
adverbial >>> pages 20–1

> In traditional grammars, a clause had to have a **finite verb**.
> Some contemporary grammars, however, define sentence
> units with non-finite verbs as clauses:
>
> They decided *to visit Paris first*
> *Going back* is always a mistake

finite and non-finite verbs >>> pages 56–7

The following sentences are each made up of two clauses. The verbs have been highlighted:

1 All animals *are* equal, 2 but some animals *are* more equal than others.

1 The headmaster *said* 2 you *ruled* them with a rod of iron.

1 Well, if I *called* the wrong number, 2 why did you *answer* the phone?

1 Because the world *is* round, 2 it *blows* my mind.

1 As Scrooge *looked* fixedly at this phenomenon, 2 it *was* a knocker again.

1 It *was* nearly night 2 when they *crossed* over

1 You *know* 2 his father*'s* vicar of a country village?

All the verbs highlighted in these clauses are known as **main verbs**.

- A clause hardly ever has more than one main verb. The rule is: *one clause – one main verb.*

- The term *main verb* can be used in two ways. Verbs can be 'main' as distinct from 'auxiliary':

    I *will* (auxiliary) *see* (main) him.

    or 'main' as distinct from 'subordinate':

    I *saw* (main) him after I *had finished* (subordinate) my newspaper.

> A **phrase** is a group of words which acts as a unit, but is not a clause.

These units from the previous sentence are all phrases:

A phrase / a group of words / as a unit / not a clause

Auxiliary verbs 22

> **Auxiliary verbs 'help' the main verb to convey a particular meaning.**

In a verb phrase such as *might have been thinking*, the main verb is the one that expresses the most important part of the meaning – in this case *thinking*. The other verbs – *might have been* – are auxiliary verbs, helping the main verb to express a particular meaning.

There are not many auxiliary verbs. They include forms of *be*, *have*, *do*, *may* and *can*.

In the following clauses the *main* and <u>auxiliary</u> verbs have been highlighted:

> But surely, Mr Worthing, you <u>have been</u> *christened* already?
>
> ...a hope that she <u>might be</u> *prevailed* upon to favour them again
>
> I <u>could</u> *put* myself in Gussie's place ... he <u>should have</u> *had* sense enough to see that he <u>was</u> *throwing* a spanner into the works

An **auxiliary verb** can be one of the following:
- part of the verbs *have*, *do* or *be* – often used to express the timing of events:

> ...when they *are* speaking, they *do* not know what they *are* saying; and when they *have* sat down, they *do* not know what they *have* said.
>
> I *have* drunk and seen the spider
>
> I*'ve been* working like a dog

52

- part of the verb *be* used to form the passive:

> You'll *be* found...
>
> We *were* put to Dickens as children, but it never quite took.

passive >>> pages 84–5

- a **modal verb**, such as *may, will, shall, might, can, should* or *must*:

> Then you *should* say what you mean...

modal verbs >>> page 54

Modal verbs

> A **modal verb** is a kind of auxiliary verb which expresses a judgement or possibility; or the idea of obligation or freedom to act.

There are nine **modal auxiliary verbs**:

shall / should
will / would
can / could
may / might
must

Examples are:

We *shall* overcome

My friend *should*, perhaps, have taken you along with him

Will you still need me, *will* you still feed me...?

I *would* / Love you ten years before the Flood

He *can* run but he *can't* hide

You *could* go on picking them...

If I *may* make a suggestion, sir...

And the hand *might* be the hand of a little child

...we *must* report that man to the police station

marginal modal verbs >>> page 57

Agreement

> Agreement is the relationship between one word in a clause or phrase and another. It is sometimes called concord. Words which show agreement with other words change their form to indicate their relationship.

The most common example of agreement can be seen in **present tense verbs**, which always agree with the **subject**:

- a singular subject takes a singular verb:

  the early <u>bird</u> *catches* the worm

- a plural subject takes a plural verb:

  early <u>birds</u> *catch* worms

There is also agreement between **demonstratives** (*this*, *that*, *these* and *those*) and **nouns**. A demonstrative has to agree in **number** (singular or plural) with the noun:

this boy / these boys
that girl / those girls

Finite and non-finite verbs

> The finite form of the verb is the one most widely used. It shows agreement with the subject and indicates tense.

agreement >>> page 55

For example, in the finite form there is a difference between:

- *I write* and *she writes*
  (different forms for the **first and third person**)
- *he writes* and *they write*
  (different forms for **singular and plural**)
- *we write* and *we wrote*
  (different forms for **present and past tense**)

Sometimes a verb phrase will have a series of verbs, made up of a main verb and its auxiliaries:

You *have been listening* to...

I'*ll be revenged* on the whole pack of you!

When this happens, the finite verb is always the first verb in the series.

> **The non-finite forms of the verb do not show agreement or indicate tense.**

One common non-finite form of the verb is the **infinitive**.

The infinitive is used:
- with **modal auxiliary** verbs:

  it <u>might</u> *be*, he <u>can</u> *run*, we <u>must</u> *report* it, we <u>shall</u> *overcome*

modal auxiliaries >>> page 53

and can be used:
- with **marginal modal** verbs (*need, ought, dare, used* [*to*]):

  Do I <u>dare to</u> *eat* a peach?

  Things we <u>used to</u> *say*

  Am I in Market Harborough? Where <u>ought</u> I <u>to</u> *be*?

Marginal modals are sometimes called **semi-modal** verbs.

The infinitive is often found with the word *to*:

To sleep, perchance *to dream*...

This is sometimes called the *to-* **infinitive**. Without *to* it can be known as the **bare infinitive**:

You made me *love* you

Participles

26

> A **participle** is the form of the verb which ends in
> either *-ing* or (in regular verbs) *-ed*.

The present participle

The present participle (which ends in *–ing*) is used:

- with the auxiliary *be*, to form a version of the present tense called the **progressive continuous**:

  She'll be *coming* round the mountain

verb tenses >>> pages 80–1
verb aspects >>> pages 82–3

- as the **verb** in an *–ing* clause:

  Lower your head before *leaving* your seat

- as an **adjective**:

  ...the last *fading* smile of a cosmic Cheshire cat

- as a **noun**:

  And the end of all our *exploring*...

This verbal noun is called a **gerund** in older grammars.

When a participial clause is not clearly related to the main clause, unfortunate ambiguities can occur:

Cruising along the Cretan coast, crusader castles are imposing and spectacular...

This construction is sometimes called the **hanging** or **dangling participle**.

The past participle

The past participle in regular verbs ends in *-ed*. For example:

look / *looked*   need / *needed*   sort / *sorted*

The past participles of irregular verbs can end in a number of ways. For example:

write / *written*	know / *known*
take / *taken*	teach / *taught*
hit / *hit*	bring / *brought*
swim / *swum*	buy / *bought*

The past participle is used:
● with the auxiliary *have* to form a version of the past tense called the **perfect**:

You<u>'ve</u> *missed* the point completely, Julia

verb tenses >>> pages 80–1

● with the auxiliary *be* to express the **passive**:

No Englishman <u>is</u> ever fairly *beaten*

When the participle is used like this, it is sometimes called the **passive participle**.

passive >>> pages 84–5

- as an **adjective**, either before or after the noun or pronoun:

  The *wounded* <u>surgeon</u> plies the steel

  When <u>you</u>'re *wounded* and left on Afghanistan's plains

- as a **noun**:

  'For the *Fallen*'

Many modern grammars do not use the terms 'present' and 'past' participles, given that the present participle is often used in past constructions:

As I was *going* to St Ives...

and the past participle is often used in present or future constructions:

Which will be *remembered* for a very long time

Simple and compound sentences 27

Most sentences can be described as **simple**, **compound** or **complex**.

Simple sentences

A **simple sentence** contains only one **clause**.

All animals are equal.
I remember it well.
Familiarity breeds contempt.

clauses >>> pages 50–1

Compound sentences

A **compound sentence** is a sentence with two or more main clauses usually joined by one of the conjunctions *and, or* or *but*.

clause A		clause B
He called for his pipe	*and*	he called for his bowl
Last week I went to Philadelphia	*but*	it was closed
Either the well was very deep	*or*	she fell very slowly

- Each of the clauses in a compound sentence could usually function independently as a simple sentence.
- The words *or, and* or *but* which link clauses in compound sentences are known as **co-ordinating conjunctions**: they usually connect units of equal status and function.

Complex sentences 28

A **complex sentence** consists of a main clause and one or more **subordinate clauses**. The main clause is the most important, or only, clause in the sentence.

subordinate clauses >>> pages 64–5

In a complex sentence, one clause is **subordinated** to the other: the subordinate clause is less important grammatically than the main clause:

And you can get it *if you try*

What happens *when you come to the beginning again*?

I don't know *where I lived before then*

Police later claimed *that a key witness had lied.*

Do not open your door *unless the caller shows some identification.*

The singer swears *(that) she has retired for good this time.*

As the water comes to the boil, add the rice.

The yeti *(if indeed it exists at all)* is unquestionably elusive.

Nero fiddled *while Rome burned.*

Subordinate clauses 29

> A **subordinate clause** is one which cannot stand as a complete sentence on its own.

Subordinate clauses are also sometimes known as **dependent clauses**. This is because they are grammatically dependent upon, as well as subordinated to, the main clause.

The subordinate clause will often be found at the beginning of the sentence:

When you got it, flaunt it

As I was going to St Ives, I met a man with seven wives.

If it moves, salute it.

There are three main types of subordinate clause:

● complement clauses:

That is *what I thought*

complement clauses >>> page 19

● relative clauses:

…all about the girl *who came to stay*

relative clauses >>> page 71

● adverbial clauses:

Will you still love me *when I'm sixty-four?*

adverbial clauses >>> pages 72–5

Subordinate clauses sometimes occur as minor sentences:

When did you meet this man?

As I was going to St Ives

Subordinating conjunctions

> In a complex sentence the subordinate clause is usually introduced by a **subordinating conjunction**.

Subordinating conjunctions connect clauses of *unequal* status and function. The clause they introduce is *subordinated* to another clause.

- **Simple subordinators** consist of one word. They include *because, if, when, as, whenever, although, though, until, while, unless, before, since* and *whereas*.

Make hay <u>while</u> the sun shines

- **Complex subordinators** are made up of more than one word, e.g. *in order that, insofar as, assuming that, in case*:

Keep a copy <u>in case</u> the original goes astray.

- **Correlative subordinators** consist of pairs of words which link two parts of the sentence, e.g. *scarcely...than, rather...than, as...as*:

<u>Scarcely</u> has Byers got over one crisis <u>than</u> another rears its head.

Minor sentences 30

> **Minor sentences are ones which do not conform to a regular pattern of subject plus verb.**

All the sentences quoted on pages 62–3 can be defined as **major sentences**. This simply means that they are made up of clauses in the regular way.

sentences >>> pages 8–9

Minor sentences are ones which are not made up of clauses, or use clauses in abnormal ways. These three make up the opening to Dickens's *Bleak House*:

> London. Michaelmas term lately over, and the Lord Chancellor sitting in Lincoln's Inn Hall. Implacable November weather.

Minor sentences are extremely common, especially in spoken English.

Types of minor sentence include:
- exclamations and interjections:

> Oh my! What a day!

- headings and signs:

> The Science Museum
>
> Getting started
>
> Where to eat in York

- abbreviated forms:

  Wish you were here
  Never fails

- greetings, replies and social formulas:

  Good morning
  Fine, thanks
  On the bus!

- proverbial sayings (aphorisms):

  More haste, less speed
  Like father, like son
  Third time lucky

Spoken conversations and dialogue in fiction are often made up almost wholly of minor sentences. These are sometimes also known as **sentence fragments**.

'He did, did he? He specifically recommended that definite costume?'
'*Yes.*'
'*Ha!*'
'*Eh?*'
'*Nothing. Just "Ha!"*'

Noun clauses

31

> A **noun clause** has the same function as a single noun or noun phrase: it can act as the subject of the sentence, the object or the complement.

nouns and noun phrases >>> pages 24–5

Noun clause as subject

Just like a noun or noun phrase, a noun clause can be the subject of the sentence:

- single noun as subject:

Wenger angered Ferguson

- noun phrase as subject:

Wenger's comment angered Ferguson

- noun clause as subject:

What Wenger said angered Ferguson

subject >>> pages 12–13

The noun clause as subject usually precedes the main verb:

That Jagger misses the limelight <u>is</u> obvious.

Noun clause as object

A noun clause can also be the object of the verb:

- noun phrase as object:

Brown has blocked *Blair's efforts*

- noun clause as object:

Brown has blocked *what Blair was striving for*

object >>> pages 16–17

Noun clause as complement

A noun clause can also act as the complement:

- noun phrase as complement:

  That was *her reply*

- noun clause as complement:

  That was *what she said*

complement >>> pages 18–19

In some sentences with noun clauses, linking words such as *that* are omitted:

I believe *you have eyes in the back of your head*

There is a fourth function of the noun clause known as the:

Noun clause in apposition

For example:

> Short's threat *that she will quit* has to be taken seriously

Here, the noun clause *that she will quit* is placed in apposition to (and expands upon) the noun phrase *Short's threat*.

Further examples are:

> The rumour *that Kylie had wed* spread like wildfire
>
> The idea *that a new stadium would be the answer to their troubles* was always questionable.

nouns in apposition >>> pages 30–1

- For a noun clause or noun phrase to be in apposition, it has to refer to the same thing as the preceding noun phrase. In the examples above:

  Short's threat was *that she would quit*

  the rumour concerned *Kylie's marriage*

  the idea was to do with *a new stadium*

- Noun clauses in apposition often begin with *that*.

Relative clauses

32

> A **relative clause** is a subordinate clause which modifies the noun in a sentence.

Relative clauses:
- follow the nouns they modify
- are normally introduced by the relative pronouns *who*, *whom*, *whose*, *which* and *that*:

Michael Caine, <u>*who*</u> *once thrilled us as Harry Palmer*, is now to play Austin Powers' pa

I spoke to the fellow *to* <u>*whom*</u> *the jewel was given*

Geri, <u>*whose*</u> *latest single flopped disastrously*, was not available for comment

The pills, <u>*which*</u> *have been on the market for over a year*, are now to be withdrawn.

This is the man, sir, <u>*that*</u> *did rescue me*.

It is common for relative clauses not to have any introductory pronoun at all:

This is the house *Jack built*

Some grammars distinguish between **restrictive** relative clauses (which narrow down a range of possibilities) and **non-restrictive** relative clauses (which add information):

The man who lives next door gets up early.   **restrictive**

The postman, who lives next door, gets up early. **non-rest**

In the first example, *the man* is being distinguished from other possible men; in the second, *who lives next door* simply gives more information about the postman.

parenthetical commas >>> page 96

Adverbial clauses 33

> **Adverbial clauses** are a type of subordinate clause which can modify verbs, adjectives or other adverbs.

Traditional grammars identify different types of adverbial clause, each introduced by its own set of subordinating conjunctions.

- The examples on the following pages show:
  - the different types of adverbial clause
  - the subordinating conjunctions which introduce them

  subordinating conjunctions >>> page 65

  - the role they play in the sentence

- **adverbial clause of time** (Typical subordinating conjunctions are *when, whenever, since, as, until* and *till*.)

> _As_ Dad came in I jumped on him from behind the door
>
> You'll stay here _until the culprit owns up_
>
> It had been there _since the estate was first built_
>
> _When_ he's found out he gets this mournful look

Adverbial clauses of time answer the question *When?*

- **adverbial clause of manner** (Typical subordinating conjunctions are *as if* and *as*.)

  > He stared vacantly, <u>*as if*</u> *he had something on his mind*
  > Just do <u>*as*</u> *I say*

  Adverbial clauses of manner answer the question *How?*

- **adverbial clause of place** (Typical subordinating conjunctions are *where* and *wherever*.)

  > She'll find it <u>*wherever*</u> *it's hidden*
  > You'll sit <u>*where*</u> *I tell you*

  Adverbial clauses of place answer the question *Where?*

- **adverbial clause of condition** (Typical subordinating conjunctions are *if* and *unless*.)

  > I'll call for you <u>*if*</u> *it stops raining*
  > We can't do it <u>*unless*</u> *he turns up with the money*

  Adverbial clauses of condition answer the question *In what circumstances?*

- **adverbial clause of concession** (Typical subordinating conjunctions are *although*, *though* and *however*.)

  > <u>*Although*</u> *the evidence is against you*, I'll accept your story
  > He was always going to fail, <u>*however*</u> *hard he worked at school*

  Adverbial clauses of concession answer the question *Despite what?*

- **adverbial clause of cause or reason** (Typical subordinating conjunctions are *as*, *because* and *since*.)

> I wish she looked fiercer _as she couldn't frighten anyone at all_
> …and then went home, _because my headache was getting worse_
> …which I found peculiar, _since I thought fabric was material_

Adverbial clauses of cause answer the question *Why?*

- **adverbial clause of purpose** (Typical subordinating conjunctions are *so that* and *in order that*.)

> I hid it _so that you wouldn't be found out!_

Adverbial clauses of purpose answer the question *With what purpose in mind?*

- **adverbial clause of result** (Typical subordinating conjunctions are *so…that* and *so that*.)

> It was _so_ wet _that we were allowed to stay in during break_
> I kept piling them up, _so that in the end the whole lot collapsed_

Adverbial clauses of result answer the question *With what result or outcome?*

- **adverbial clause of degree** (Typical subordinating conjunctions are *as…as* and *than*.)

> I ate _as_ much _as I could_
> He wanted it more _than I did_

Adverbial clauses of degree answer the question *To what extent?*

When the adverbial clause precedes the main clause, it is common practice to punctuate with a comma.

comma >>> pages 90–1

Verb moods

> **Moods** are different forms of the verb. Their function is to affect the general meaning of the sentence.

The most common moods are the **indicative** and the **imperative**.

- **the indicative** (or **declarative**) **mood**
  This is used for 'indicating' or 'declaring' things to do with facts. The verbs in statements and questions are in the indicative mood:

  Harry Potter *was* a highly unusual boy in many ways

  Did you really *blow up* your aunt, Harry?

In some grammars, questions are said to be in the **interrogative mood**.

- **the imperative mood**
  This form is used to express – among other things –
  commands, requests and warnings:

  Swear to me that whatever you might hear –
  Please *take* a seat!
  Watch out!

imperative mood >>> pages 78–9

Still used in French, but uncommon in English is **the
subjunctive mood**. The subjunctive form can be used to
express conditions, uncertainty and wishes:

I wouldn't go in there, if I *were* you
We suggest that she *leave* immediately
I wish he *were* here.

modal verbs >>> page 54

The imperative 35

> The **imperative** is the mood of the verb used to express – among other things – commands and requests.

The imperative is used in **directive** sentences. Directives are used when we want to:

● command:

Take three a day after meals
Go away!

● request:

Please enclose a cheque with each order
Do have a seat

● warn:

Look out!
Mind your head

● offer:

Have one more wafer-thin mint

● plead:

Help!

● invite:

Come to our house-warming

● instruct:

Take the third on the left

- advise:

  Have a few minutes' rest

- express good wishes:

  Enjoy your birthday!

The subject of an imperative sentence is usually *you*. But this pronoun is normally omitted, except in emphatic directives:

You do as you're told!   You be quiet!   You just wait!

Some imperative sentences can have a first- or third-person pronoun as the subject:

Now let *me* see...   *Let's* get out of here!
Everyone leave immediately!   *Nobody* say a word!

Verb tenses

> The different **tense** forms of the verb express the
> time at which an action took place or a state of
> affairs prevailed.

One function of verbs is to indicate three basic times: present,
past and future. To do this, they have different forms, known as
tenses.

'...oh, I *beg* your pardon,'	**present**
cried Alice again...	**past**
'We *won't talk* about her any more...'	**future**

The present tense
This is normally used to describe events happening or states
prevailing at the time at which the speaker or writer is actually
speaking or writing:

I *need* a drink

The past tense
- The **simple past** (sometimes called the **preterite**) is
  formed with *-ed* in regular verbs:

  And the pig got up and slowly *walked* away.

  In that sentence, *got* is an example of the simple past in an
  irregular verb: *get*.

- The auxiliary verb *have/had* can be used to form versions of
  the past tense. In some grammars, these are called the
  perfect and **pluperfect**:

I *have tasted* eggs, certainly...	**perfect**
By this time she *had found* her way into a tiny little room...	**pluperfect**

past perfective >>> page 83

- There is also a form of the past which uses the marginal modal *used to*:

> ...we *used to* call him Tortoise

In Latin, this would be called the **imperfect**.

marginal modal verbs >>> page 57

The future

The term 'tense' actually refers to the way the verb changes its endings.

The form of the verb does not change to express the future. Instead, to express future time, we use the auxiliary verbs *will* and *shall*, and the form *be going*:

> I *shall* give you my answer in the morning.
>
> You *will* never succeed
>
> We*'ll* regret this
>
> They*'re going* to open a new branch

The fact that the verb does not change its form to indicate the future causes some grammarians to say that, strictly speaking, there is no such thing as a future tense.

The future, however, can be thought of as a **compound tense**, requiring an auxiliary verb.

Verb aspects 37

> The **aspects** of the verb express different ways of looking at the timing of an event or situation – for example, its duration or repetition.

A verb can have **simple**, **progressive** or **perfective** aspects.

The simple aspect
The simple aspect suggests that an activity is complete:

I *ran* the London marathon.

Shakespeare *died* in 1616.

She *makes* a swift exit.

The progressive aspect
The progressive aspect:
- expresses the idea that someone is in the middle of doing something
- uses the auxiliary verb *be* with the *-ing* participle:

I *'m leaving.* He *was snoring.* They *'ve been laughing* at me.

participles >>> pages 58–61

The **present progressive** (or **present continuous**) shows that an event is in progress at the time of speaking and not yet completed:

I*'m opening out* like the largest telescope that ever was…

The **past progressive** (or **past continuous**) shows that an event was in progress at a certain time:

Alice *was beginning* to get very tired of sitting by her sister on the bank…

The perfective aspect

The perfective aspect:

- shows that an action in the past has a result *now*
- uses the auxiliary verb *have* with the *past participle*:

  I *'ve seen* enough. They *had missed* their chance.

The **present perfective** aspect is used to refer to an event which started in the past and is still continuing into the present:

  I *have not slept* for three hundred years ... and I am so tired.

The **past perfective** aspect is used to refer to an event which had started in the past and was still continuing:

  He *had hardly gone* a couple of miles when he heard somebody galloping after him...

pluperfect >>> page 80

The perfective and progressive aspects can combine to produce meanings such as:

The club *has been going* downhill for a long time

(present perfective progressive)

I *will have been working* for sixty years next October

(future perfective progressive)

He *had been jabbering* madly but now fell silent

(past perfective progressive)

Active and passive

38

> In an **active** sentence, the subject performs the action; in a **passive** sentence, the subject is on the receiving end of the action.

subject >>> pages 12–13

For example:

> Henman [s] *defeated* [active v] the Croatian in straight sets.
>
> Henman [s] *was defeated* [passive v] in the next round.

The passive can be used:

● when the receiver of the action is more important than the doer:

> The eighty-one-year-old *was struck* by a car on her way home

● when the doer is not known:

> Fry's Oxfordshire mansion *was burgled* some time on Tuesday

● when the doer is unimportant:

> Bicycles must not *be left* in the entrance hall

● when the doer is obvious:

> Lincoln *was* swiftly *re-elected*

- in scientific writing which needs to be impersonal:

  The substance *was subjected* to a battery of tests

- when the writer does not want to reveal who the doer is:
  o to maintain suspense:

  The handle *was turned* slowly from the inside...

  o to avoid having to name the agents:

  Eleven civilians *were killed* in Thursday's raid

  o in an attempt to leave details unclear:

  We were assured that the crops *had been* properly *trialled*

- Writers do not always follow their own advice. These two statements from George Orwell appear in the same essay:

Never use the passive where you *can use* the active.   **active**
The passive *is ... used* in preference to...   **passive**

- Some grammars refer to the active and passive **voice**.

Ending the sentence   39

> The ends of most sentences in print are marked with
> a full stop (or full point), **question mark** or
> **exclamation mark**.

The full stop

The full stop is by far the commonest of the marks used to
indicate the end of a sentence:

Marley's face.

Squire Trelawney, Dr Livesey, and the rest of these
gentlemen having asked me to write down the whole
particulars about Treasure Island, from the beginning to the
end, keeping nothing back but the bearings of the island,
and that only because there is still treasure not lifted, I take
up my pen in the year of grace 17—, and go back to the
time when my father kept the "Admiral Benbow" inn, and
the brown old seaman, with the sabre cut, first took up his
lodging under our roof.

It can also be used to mark:
- an abbreviated word or phrase:

Dr.   O.B.E.   Ms.   e.g.   q.v.   B.Sc.

- times and dates:

7.40   19.2.02

- decimals and money:

1.5 + 2.49   £3.60   €5.00

- sections in a written text:

see paragraph 2.2   (*Henry V*, 1.2.242)

- The full stop can also be called a **full point** and is known as **period** in American English.
- Punctuation in American and British English can follow different style conventions.
- In British English, full stops are not usually found in common abbreviations such as BBC and NATO.
- There are different styles of punctuation. For example, the full stops in the abbreviations above (Dr. etc) are typical of **heavy punctuation** and would be omitted in **light punctuation**.

The question mark

- The question mark is used at the end of an interrogative word, phrase or sentence:

> 'Becky, d'you think you're a boy? Eh?'
> 'Why?'

- The question mark can show that a sentence is a question, even though the phrasing might imply that it is a statement:

> So now it's OK to swear in front of your mother?

- A statement with a brief question added on to the end is called a **tag question**. The added interrogative element is the **question tag**:

> I'd just ride away with them, *wouldn't I*?
> Given themselves a name as well, *have they*?
> It's OK, *isn't it*?

- Question tags can also be used with directives, where they often end with an exclamation mark:

> Just wait a minute, *will you*!

directives >>> pages 78–9

- The question mark can be called the **interrogation mark** or **interrogation point** in American English.

The exclamation mark

The exclamation mark has a variety of linked uses, seen in these quotations from Ben Elton's *Gridlock*. It can be used for:

- exclamations:

'Aaaargh! We've got a sicko!' screamed Dolores

- commands:

'Go away! I mean, come back!'

- strong assertions:

'No!' said Sam incredulously

- emotions such as surprise or contempt:

'Saints preserve us, what a joke!'

- powerful personal feelings:

'Another year goes by! And still he hasn't come!'

- forceful speech in dialogue:

'Hear me! Hear me!' thundered Big Beard

Fiction writers and journalists occasionally use multiple exclamation marks for effect:

'Britain has hundreds and hundreds of miles of canals! ... Today, we carry coal by road!!!'

The comma

> The **comma** is a punctuation mark used to separate words, phrases or clauses.

The comma has a number of uses (here illustrated by Bill Bryson):
- to divide off elements in a sequence of words or phrases:

> I had never heard of Tesco's, Perthshire, council houses, Morecambe and Wise, railway cuttings…
>
> A packet of crisps was 5p, a soft drink 8p, lipstick 45p, chocolate biscuits 12p, an iron £4.50…

- to indicate a parenthesis (added material within a clause):

> It would be, in short, one of the most extraordinary years in modern British history.

parenthesis >>> pages 96–9

- to separate clauses:

> Before the day was half over, I knew that this was where I wanted to be.

relative clauses >>> page 71

It is usual to use a comma after a subordinate clause if the subordinate clause starts the sentence:

> Before the night was over, the moon had vanished.

but if the order of the clauses is reversed, the comma is not normally included:

> The moon had vanished before the night was over.

In a sentence like this example, the insertion of a comma helps us avoid misreading the sentence (in this case as 'over the moon').

- in direct speech:

'The minimum stay,' she went on, 'is five nights at one pound a night...'

speech punctuation >>> pages 108–15

- to add a brief pause for emphasis:

He spoke slowly, and deliberately.

- to clarify meaning:

Inside, another new world opened for me.

(The comma prevents us from reading the sentence as: *Inside another new world...*)

- with vocatives (the person or persons to whom the sentence is addressed):

Bert, take a look at this!

- The comma can also be used:
  - in numerals, to mark off thousands:

  20,000 Leagues under the Sea

  - in letter writing:

  Dear Helene,   Sincerely, Frank

- Most writers do not place a comma before *and* in a list:

  ...with busy rooflines, spacious verandas, odd-sized windows and acres of trailing roses...

The comma is commonly found before *and* in American English, however.

> The **semi-colon** (;) allows a writer to join two
> sentences on the same subject into one sentence. It
> also provides a stronger division in a sentence that is
> already punctuated with commas.

The semi-colon can be used:
- to link statements that are closely associated in meaning, or complement each other in some way:

  They are incapable of walking; their stubby limbs wave
  around helplessly if they lose contact with their mother in
  the burrow.

- to separate clauses of equal weight in a co-ordinated sentence:

  Severe pain, muscle seizure and heart failure may end in
  rapid death; or the pain may be so intense that the victim is
  unable to swim and drowns.

- to separate long items in a description or list, particularly when some of the items themselves contain commas:

> Her matted, filthy black hair hung down to her shoulders; her jagged claws gripped the stone fiercely; her powerful dark wings were folded along her back...

> You need a pound of potatoes which have already been lightly boiled; a grated onion; three cloves of garlic, freshly pressed; and a teaspoonful of Dijon mustard...

- to mark a stronger division, or longer pause, than a comma:

> The fine ashes fall, covering everything; slowly, insidiously

- to mark off a series of complex points:

> On this scale, the Sun is but a week old; its flaming youth will continue for another month; then it will settle down to a sedate adult existence which may last at least eighty years

---

A semi-colon is used to join two complete sentences into a single written sentence when:
1 the two sentences are felt to be too closely related in meaning to be separated by a full stop
2 there is no connecting word which would require a comma, such as *and* or *but*
3 a colon would not be appropriate

colon >>> pages 94–5

Punctuation can be a subjective business. For example, in the first quotation on page 92, the writer could have used a colon instead of a semi-colon. While the two are certainly not interchangeable, their use depends on the connection that the writer intends to make between the two clauses. Equally, the clauses in the first quotation above might, in another writer's hands, have been separated by commas.

The colon 42

The **colon** (:) shows that there is something to follow in the sentence. It has a wide variety of linked uses.

Expanding and explaining

The colon can be used:

- to expand or develop the point made in the opening clause:

Her face was smooth and unwrinkled, but aged beyond even the age of the witches: she had seen thousands of years pass, and the cruelty and misery of all of them had formed the hateful expression on her features.

- to explain or complement the point in the opening clause:

Their end, when it came, was very different from that of their victims: swift and relatively painless.

Lead-ins

The colon can also be used:

- to lead from an introduction to a theme:

> The key question was: would a jury be willing to send two men to the gallows on fingerprint evidence?

> These four observations led him to one conclusion: most of the young animals must die, and the ones that survived were best fitted to their way of life.

- to lead from statement to example:

> There were too many problems: to start with, Beckham wasn't fully fit.

- to lead from cause to effect:

> The key players were missing: the team lost heart.

- to lead from premise to conclusion:

> The finches had different beaks: they must have developed separately.

- to lead into a 'punch-line':

> In the second half, two things happened: a dog ran on to the pitch and Tambling scored a goal

- to introduce a list of items in formal writing:

> You will need: a detailed map of the area, a compass…

In informal writing, there could be no punctuation after *need*.

- to introduce speech:

> Of her MBE, she added: 'I feel very honoured…'

> When you look at it, you say: this is the mesozoic lawnmower

> Serafina Pekkala said to the lost dæmon: 'Did you say there are still some witches helping these people?'

> LISTER: So?

Parenthesis

> A **parenthesis** is a word, phrase or clause, inserted into the sentence to provide additional information.

Any material in parenthesis is not grammatically essential to the sentence, which would be complete without it. For example:

Aisle seven ('Food for the Seriously Obese') was especially productive.

> Aisle seven was especially productive.

A parenthesis can be marked in three ways, by pairs of:
- commas
- brackets
- dashes

Commas for parenthesis

Commas are used when the material in the parenthesis does not need to stand out as being especially important:

The outcome, however, was very different.

Dyer, who had replaced Hargreaves, was constantly off the pace

comma >>> pages 90–1

Parenthetical commas can be used to avoid ambiguity in relative clauses:

My girlfriend, who lives in Doncaster, usually travels down by train.

Without commas, the speaker appears to be distinguishing between his many girlfriends.

relative clauses >>> page 71

Brackets for parenthesis

Round brackets are used when the writer wants to draw attention to the parenthesis. They are useful for:

- explanations:

> Gemini compensates for the blurring of images (star twinkle) caused by the Earth's atmosphere by using adaptive optics (AO) instruments

- additional information:

> They ordered ... Empire biscuits (they had been called German biscuits before the war).

- comments:

> Every occupied tent has a pair of muddy legs sticking out the front door (can't be bothered to take the boots off), with people trying to keep the inside clean

- asides:

> When the other little Zetas agreed to comply, I bit the head off the jelly-baby (orange was my favourite) and I think I offered the rest of it to the captured Zeta

Although commas, dashes and brackets are often interchangeable (see note on page 101), in the examples on this page, commas would not be appropriate.

● afterthoughts:

I had a vague recollection of having glimpsed something furry on the bottom shelf towards the back. (Turned out to be a large piece of Gorgonzola.)

● facts and references:

Monroe, Marilyn (1926–1962)

● stage directions:

KRYTEN: Sir, I think you should take a look at this. (*Holds out Lister's ID card.*)

● **Round brackets** are themselves sometimes called **parentheses**.
● **Square brackets** are often used when someone who is not the writer of the original text needs to add a comment or explanation:

…he was a relative of the Marshall Pelisser [commander of the allied French army]…

● They are also used widely in reference books:

BRACKETS [16c: from the singular *bragget* and *braget*, from French *braguette* a codpiece] another term for…

Dashes for parenthesis

Dashes are used when a writer wants a parenthesis to stand out with greater emphasis than would be achieved with commas or brackets:

Det Insp Charles Collins, also of the Fingerprint Branch – which by now had 90,000 prints on file – wanted to get fingerprints accepted by the courts.

When it walked – at an estimated 4.25 mph – it had a stride of 2.7 metres.

...and beneath where I stood, I could see – what the Russians could not – steadily drawn up, quiet and expectant, the squadrons of English and French cavalry...

The correct answer – that the bomb will hit the ground more or less directly below the point at which the aircraft has arrived at the moment of impact – is often rejected.

The dash 44

> The dash has a variety of uses. For example, as well as indicating parenthesis, it can be used when adding a further statement or afterthought, or to show that an utterance is incomplete.

The dash is used:
- to indicate an additional statement which makes an important point:

  For now I am a judge – and a good judge too!

- in the place of a colon when the writer wants to give emphasis to a concluding statement by inserting a dramatic pause:

  One pattern of ridges belonged to an unidentified person – the murderer.

colon >>> pages 94–5

- to show an interrupted or incomplete utterance in dialogue:

  'Ali,' said Roger. 'Your mother's knocking around. Don't you think – ?'

- as a link, replacing 'to':

  see pages 23–45
  the London–Glasgow line
  the 1939–45 war

Though unusual in English, the dash has also been used by some authors to replace inverted commas in dialogue:

– Has your mother had a happy life?
– How do I know? Stephen said.
– How many children had she?
– Nine or ten, Stephen answered. Some died.

- The dash is now commonly used to replace other punctuation marks in informal writing and emails:

  Bill –
  we found the car – completely wrecked – total write-off

- In some older texts, longer dashes were widely used:
  ○ to indicate that a piece of information had been withheld:

  'From Lowood School, in —shire.'

  I take up my pen in the year of grace 17—,

  ○ to avoid writing taboo words in full:

  "D—n Milton!" answered the squire.

- In this last use, dashes are now often replaced by asterisks:

  Shopping and F***ing

- In many of the examples of parenthesis, commas, brackets and dashes are almost interchangeable: the choice of punctuation is influenced by the extent to which the words in parenthesis need to stand out.

The hyphen 45

The main use of the **hyphen** is to join whole words and elements of words to form longer words and compounds. Used in this way, it is known as the **link hyphen**.

The link hyphen can be found, for example, in:

- occupations: *lorry-driver, tax-inspector, sheep-farmer*
- mixed roles: *player-manager, actor-director, singer-songwriter*
- national and regional combinations: *Anglo-French, Franco-Prussian, Indo-European*
- places with a purpose: *boiler-room, filling-station, chip-shop*
- physical descriptions: *brown-eyed, two-year-old, knock-kneed*
- scientific terms: *radio-isotope, infra-red, bi-metallic, ozone-friendly*

and a variety of other linked concepts, such as: *non-fiction, part-time, anti-establishment, tough-guy, hang-gliding, hand-writing, word-processing, cooking-apples, labour-saving, house-plants, English-speaking, drugs-related, weed-infested.*

- The link hyphen is sometimes used to avoid ambiguity. For example, we might both *recover* and *re-cover* a lost umbrella.
- Words with confusing letter-combinations can also be clarified by a hyphen: *co-operate, re-use, de-acidify.*
- Many compound words, including some of those above, are frequently written without the hyphen, so that we find, for example: *bimetallic* and *word processing.* This is especially common in American English.
- The use of the hyphen is often subjective and dependent upon context. For example, it is possible to find *book case, book-case* and *bookcase.*

The hyphen used to mark the division of a word at the end of a line of print is known as the **break hyphen**. This is usually only used when text is right-justified:

> Grammar books typically go into great detail about the formation of sen-tences and of the smaller units (such as clauses and phrases) that they con-tain, but say very little...

There are no fixed rules concerning the position of the break hyphen: some writers are happy to break at any syllables (*cir-cumstance*); others strictly according to etymology (*circum-stance*).

Ideally the break hyphen should pass unnoticed. It would be possible, for example, to find *int-ernational, inter-national, internat-ional* or *internation-al* — but probably not a division such as *inte-rnational*.

The apostrophe to show possession

46

> The apostrophe has two main uses:
> - to mark possession in nouns
> - to show that a letter or group of letters has been omitted

apostrophe to show omission >>> page 106

These are the conventions followed for the use of the apostrophe to show possession:

Apostrophe with singular nouns
- Singular nouns have *apostrophe s*:

  Schindler's List, The Goalkeeper's Revenge, a dog's life

Apostrophe with plural nouns
- Plural nouns ending in single *s* have *s apostrophe*:

  Travellers' Tales, Footballers' Wives, passengers' luggage

- Plural nouns which do not end in single *s* show possession like singular nouns, and have *apostrophe s*:

  women's rights, children's playground, men's changing room

Apostrophe with names

- Names which end in single *s* can be written either with *apostrophe s*:

Keats's poems
Jesus's parables
St Thomas's Hospital

or with just the apostrophe:

Keats' poems
Jesus' parables
St Thomas' Hospital

People's preferences for *s's* or *s'* in names like this are often determined by whether the *s* is pronounced in speech. For example, we might write *Keats's poems* (pronounced *Keatses*) but *Xerxes' army.*

- Many well-known place names and public signs, as well as the names of businesses and organisations, are written without apostrophes:

Earls Court   *Mens Wear*

Harrods   Barclays

- It is important to note that possessive pronouns do not have apostrophes:

hers, ours, its, yours, theirs

possessive pronouns >>> page 33

The apostrophe to show omission 47

The **apostrophe** can show omission, for example:
- in colloquial or informal contexts:

> *They're* the oddest new couple in pop... Geri's friends are astonished *she's* got involved... You *wouldn't* expect them to...

- in representing dialogue:

> 'My *dad'll* beat *your'n.*'

- in traditional forms such as:

> *o'clock* (of the clock), *bo'sun* (boatswain), *fo'c's'le* (forecastle – sometimes written as *fo'c'sle*)

- The apostrophe is also occasionally found in some plurals, such as letters of the alphabet or unusual constructions: *dot your i's, do's and don't's...*
- But it is used less commonly nowadays in:
  - abbreviations such as *VIPs* (traditionally written as *VIP's*)
  - centuries and decades: *the 1800s, the 1960s* (for *1800's, 1960's*)

its and it's

Confusingly, *its* (= *belonging to it*) does not have an apostrophe, even though it is a possessive. It helps to think of it as part of a set including *hers, yours* and *ours.*

> Its appetite for worms increased by the day.

The apostrophe in *it's* only indicates omission:

> *It's raining (it is...)*
> *It's been raining (it has...)*

Gaps and suspense

> **Ellipsis** is the term given to the deliberate omission of part of a text. The three dots used to show that something has been left out (…) are known as **ellipsis points**.

For example, the second sentence above could be abbreviated to:

> The three dots … are known as ellipsis points.

Ellipsis points can also be used when a writer wants to leave the sentence unfinished for dramatic effect:

> – to-morrow we will run faster, stretch out our arms further…

or to leave a picture in the reader's mind:

> His body would not be found until it had decayed so much that townsfolk started feeling poorly…

> When three dots are used to show a pause, rather than an omission, they are called **suspension points**.

For example:

> 'I just wanted to say… Sam, that you're the boss, OK? I know that Ministers of Transport may come and Ministers of Transport may go, but car builders, well, they stay forever… I know that now, it was stupid of me to forget it, and, well… I'm sorry.'

Dialogue 49

The following extract from Lewis Carroll's *Alice's Adventures in Wonderland* illustrates the conventions which are normally followed in the United Kingdom when punctuating dialogue in fiction.

The Hatter opened his eyes very wide on hearing this; but all he said was,[1] 'Why is a raven like a writing-desk?'[2]

[3]'Come, we shall have some fun now![4]' thought Alice. 'I'm glad they've begun asking riddles – I believe I can guess that,' she added aloud.

'[5]Do you mean that you think you can find out the answer to it?' [6]said the March Hare.

'Exactly so,' said Alice.

'Then you should say what you mean,' the March Hare went on.

'I do,' Alice hastily replied; 'at least – at least I mean what I say – that's the same thing, you know.'

'Not the same thing a bit!' said the Hatter. [7] 'You might as well say that [8]"I see what I eat" is the same as "I eat what I see"!'

'You might just as well say,' added the March Hare, [9] 'that "I like what I get" is the same thing as "I get what I like"!'

[1] A phrase which introduces direct speech ends in a comma or colon.

colon >>> pages 94–5

direct speech >>> page 112

[2] The speaker's actual words are placed inside **speech marks** (also called **inverted commas**, **quotation marks** or **quotes**).

[3] A new paragraph indicates a change of speaker.

[4] There must be a punctuation mark at the end of a unit of direct speech, placed before the closing speech mark.

[5] Each new speech begins with a capital letter.

[6] *said* begins with a lower-case *s*, even though it follows a question mark, because the sentence carries on.

[7] The full stop at the end of the **reporting clause** (*said the Hatter*) and capital letter (for *You*) show that the first part of the speech ('*Not the same thing a bit!*') was a completed utterance.

reporting clause >>> pages 112–13

[8] Double quotation marks (" ") are used when the writer needs to place a quote within a passage that is already enclosed by single quotation marks.

quotation marks >>> page 111

[9] The comma at the end of the reporting clause (*added the March Hare*) and lower-case letter (for *that*) show that the first part of the speech ('*You might just as well say,*') was not a completed utterance and that the sentence carries on.

Introducing speech and quotations

- A speech will usually be introduced by either a comma:

...all he said was, 'Why is a raven like a writing-desk?'

or a colon:

He exhaled thoughtfully and said: 'Put it this way. I was clean shaven when I got here.'

- A quotation, however, does not need to be introduced by a comma or colon:

The Prime Minister, who had described the Barcelona meeting as a 'make-or-break' summit...

- When speech extends over several paragraphs, each new paragraph begins with opening speech marks, but they are closed only at the very end of the quoted section.
- Clauses which indicate the participants in dialogue – such as *thought Alice, she added aloud, said Alice* and *the March Hare went on* – are called **reporting clauses**.

reporting clause >>> pages 112–13

Quotation marks 50

Singles or doubles?
- There are no fixed rules about when to use single or double quotes, but doubles are more commonly found in handwriting, in newspapers and in American publications.
- Where double inverted commas are used for speech (as they often are in newspapers), any quote-within-a-quote is placed in single inverted commas:

> But last night a senior Whitehall source said: "If this was a 'make or break' summit, then it broke."

The reverse arrangement – doubles within singles (usual in fiction) – also applies:

> 'By "proper treatment", sir, you mean – '

Titles
- Quotation marks can also be used when writing the titles of shorter works, such as articles or poems. Titles of longer works tend to be in italics:

> They had titles like 'Knit Your Own Twinset'...
>
> This place might have been lifted whole from *Adventures on the Island*.

Sneering and scaring
- Sneer quotes have a derogatory effect and can substitute for the phrase 'so called'.

> Trench 'troops' insult the real heroes of war

- Scare quotes are used here by Simon Hoggart to alert the reader to a new or unusual expression:

> ...and no fewer than three "chuggers" which, I gather, is the term for charity muggers

Direct and indirect speech

51

> Direct speech reproduces the actual words used by the speaker or writer. Indirect (or reported) speech is used when someone else is reporting what was said or written.

For example:

'Dick,' said Silver, 'I trust you.'	**direct speech**
> Silver said that he trusted Dick.	**indirect speech**

The **reporting clause** can be placed:
- before the speech:

Silver said, 'Dick, I trust you.'

- within the speech:

'Dick,' *said Silver,* 'I trust you.'

- after the speech:

'Dick, I trust you,' *said Silver.*
'Dick, I trust you,' *Silver said.*

What happens in indirect speech

Direct speech undergoes a number of changes when it is turned into indirect speech. These changes affect:

- tense
- adverbials of time and place
- pronouns

Changing tense

Verbs are generally **back-shifted** in tense:

- the present tense becomes the past:

'I *am* a mortal,' Scrooge remonstrated.	**dir**
Scrooge remonstrated that he *was* a mortal.	**ind**

verb tenses >>> pages 80–1

- the past tense is shifted back using the perfective aspect (past perfect):

'He *died* seven years ago.'	**dir**
> Scrooge added that Marley *had died* seven years before.	**ind**

verb aspects >>> pages 82–3

In some contexts the verb in the reported clause is not back-shifted. For example, there is a difference between the following:

He told me he *was* ill (back-shifted – offering the possibility that he has since recovered)
He told me he *is* ill (not back-shifted – he is still unwell)

The correct relationship between the verbs in the reporting clause (*Scrooge remonstrated*) and the reported clause (*that he was a mortal*) is called the **sequence of tenses**.

Changing adverbials of time and place

Time and place references change because the person reporting the speech is taking a different perspective.

- Time references in direct speech such as *yesterday, next year, now...* become *the previous day/the day before, the following year, then...*

'Come! Dine with us *tomorrow*!'	**dir**
> Fred asked Scrooge to dine with them *the following day*.	**ind**

- Place references such as *here, in this town...* become *there, in that town...*

'I was bred *in this place*! I was a boy *here*!'	**dir**
> Scrooge exclaimed that he had been bred *in that place*; he had been a boy *there*.	**ind**

Changing personal pronouns

- First and second person pronouns and possessives (*I, we, us, you, my, your...*) usually change to the third person (*she, he, it, her, him, they, them, his, its, their...*):

'In life *I* was *your* partner, Jacob Marley.'	**dir**
> Marley reminded Scrooge that in life *he* had been *his* partner.	**ind**

Indirect questions, exclamations and instructions

The examples on pages 112–14 are mainly direct and indirect statements. There are also:
- indirect questions
- indirect exclamations
- indirect instructions

Indirect questions

When a direct question is reported as an indirect question, there is a change in word order:

'Who *are you*?' (V + pron)	dir
> Scrooge asked the ghost who *he was*. (pron + V)	ind

Indirect questions also involve the addition of *if* or *whether*:

'You travel fast?' said Scrooge.	dir
> Scrooge asked *if/whether* the spirit travelled fast.	ind

Indirect exclamations

These are not very common, but a typical example is:

'What a strange man you are, Uncle Scrooge!'	dir
> Fred told his uncle what a strange man he was.	ind

Indirect instructions

Like indirect statements, these can require changes to verbs and pronouns:

'Tell *me* if Tiny Tim *will* live.'	dir
> Scrooge asked the spirit to tell *him* if Tiny Tim *would* live.	ind

Paragraphs 52

> A **paragraph** is a single block of text. Typically, a
> single paragraph will express one main idea or
> theme.

Dividing a piece of writing into paragraphs helps writers to
organise their thoughts. It also helps readers to identify shifts of
focus, for example in a narrative, description or argument.

A paragraph can consist of only one sentence, or of many. This
paragraph, from the opening chapter of Dickens's *Bleak House*,
follows a paragraph seven sentences long and totalling 300
words:

> Thus, in the midst of the mud and the heart of the fog, sits
> the Lord High Chancellor in his High Court of Chancery.

Paragraph length

Different forms and genres follow different conventions in terms of the lengths of paragraphs. For example, paragraphs in tabloid newspaper articles are often quite short, as in this *Sun* leader:

Muggers and junkies rule our streets. We need more jails.

We need action *NOW*.

These are strong words indeed about the state of the criminal justice system.

Paragraphs are also traditionally short in many religious texts:

How are the mighty fallen in the midst of battle!
O Jonathan, thou wast slain in thine high places.
    I am distressed for thee, my brother Jonathan: very pleasant hast thou been unto me: thy love to me was wonderful, passing the love of women.

Indentation

There are few clear-cut rules governing whether or not to indent a new paragraph.

New paragraphs are:
- usually indented in print (and always in dialogue)
- not usually indented when paragraphs are separated by a blank line space

Accent

> An **accent** is the set of pronunciation features which help to indicate a person's geographical origin and/or their social class.

Identifying accents

- In very general terms, we might talk about a 'regional' accent or a 'working-class regional' accent.
- More specifically, it is possible to identify a Glasgow accent, a 'working-class London' accent or a Cornish accent.
- Specialists, and people brought up in a particular locality, can even make fine distinctions between the accents of neighbouring communities.

Defining accents

Accents are often described by reference to two qualities: their 'music' and their vocal sounds.

- Many accents seem to have a musical quality: we talk of the 'sing-song' accent of south Wales, or a southern Irish 'lilt'.
- Accents also have vocal qualities. The Liverpool 'Scouse' accent is sometimes described as 'adenoidal', Highland Scottish accents as 'soft' and north Wales accents as 'guttural'.

Received Pronunciation

> **Received Pronunciation** (often abbreviated to RP) is the accent associated with educated speakers of British English, and the one most commonly used as a model for foreign learners.

Although frequently associated with the south-east of England, RP is spoken throughout the United Kingdom. Unlike regional accents, it tells us about a speaker's social class or educational background – not where they come from.

Like all accents, there are many variants of RP and it has changed over time.

- It has been estimated that only 3% of British English users speak RP. Most people have a mixture of RP and a regional accent, known as **modified RP**.
- The term **Estuary English** was coined in the 1980s to apply to the way in which London accents were spreading to the regions adjoining the Thames Estuary. More recently it has come to describe the accent adopted by some people as a conscious move away from RP.

Dialect 54

> A **dialect** is a variety of language used by a particular group of people, which has distinctive features of **vocabulary** and **grammar**.

For example, we might speak in general terms of 'a Yorkshire dialect' or 'the dialects of the south-west'.

Most dialects are regional dialects and, like accents, contain features which help to indicate where the speaker comes from. But, whereas accent refers to pronunciation, dialect refers to vocabulary and grammar.

For example:
● vocabulary:

> Aal except for little Geordie who wes lame an' couldn't keep up wi' the *wee bairns*.
> (Tyneside)

● grammar:

> ...so we tossed up and *him who lost* had to do it first. And I lost, oh, and *you'd to* take your socks off *an' all*. So I took my socks off, and I kept lookin' at this welli' full of taddies, and this kid kept saying, 'Go on then, *tha frightened*, tha frightened.' I was an' all.
> (Yorkshire)

The term **accent** applies only to the sounds of speech: it has nothing to do with grammar. Nonetheless, a regional accent will be linked to the dialect of that same region. For example, the Tyneside 'Geordie' accent is inseparable from the Geordie dialect.

Standard English

> Standard English is the name given to the particular dialect of English that:
> - is normally used for writing and public communication
> - is most widely understood
> - carries most prestige

'Standard English ... developed from one of the Middle English dialects (East Midlands – the dialect first printed by Caxton) to become the written form used by all writers of English, no matter which dialect area they come from. It is the fact of being the written form which establishes it as the standard.'
(The Kingman Report, 1988)

Each English-speaking country has its own standard variety, such as Standard American English (AmE) or Standard Caribbean English. The standard dialect of the United Kingdom is therefore sometimes referred to as Standard British English (BrE).

The differences between these standard dialects can be considerable, especially in their vocabularies. For example:

BrE	AmE
boot	*trunk*
petrol	*gas*
windscreen	*windshield*
bonnet	*hood*
rear light	*taillight*
aerial	*antenna*
number plate	*license plate*
accelerator	*gas pedal*
gear lever	*gear shift*
wing mirror	*side mirror*
indicator	*turn signal*

It is important to recognise that Standard English is not:
- the 'best' English
- 'proper' English
- 'upper-class' English
- the most widely used variety of English
- an 'official' variety planned and authorised by a body of linguists

- While everyone can understand Standard English, very few people use it in speech. Most people have their own way of speaking which is a mixture of standard and regional dialects. This 'personal dialect' is known as an **idiolect**.
- Standard English can be – and is – spoken in any accent. Regional dialects, on the other hand, are always spoken in the accompanying regional accent.
- All of us who speak English are dialect speakers: we all have at least one dialect.

Pidgins and creoles 56

> Pidgins and creoles are languages (rather than dialects) which have developed to allow groups who do not understand each other's language to communicate with each other.

Pidgins

Pidgin languages evolved to allow the exchange of simple information, for example when European traders made contact with African or Asian language communities.

One of the best-known examples is Tok Pisin (Papua New Guinea Pidgin English). The name might mean 'talk pidgin'. Here in Tok Pisin is the opening of Mark Antony's famous speech from *Julius Caesar.*
'Friends, Romans, countrymen, lend me your ears;
I come to bury Caesar…'

Pren, man bilong Rom, Wantok, harim nau.
Mi kam tasol long plantim Kaesar…
(Friends, men belonging to Rome, countrymen, hear now;
Me come to long-plant Caesar…)

- One interesting feature of Tok Pisin is the form of the possessive using *bilong* ('belonging to'). Thus, *Henry's house* is *haus bilong Henry.*
- Tok Pisin has now been **creolised** and is the official language of Papua New Guinea.

Creoles

When children are born who speak a pidgin language as their native tongue, it becomes a creole. In other words, a creole is a pidgin which has become the mother-tongue of a community.

An example is Jamaican creole:

> Jamaica language sweet yuh know buoy,
> An yuh know *mi nebba notice i'*,   *I never noticed it*
> Till *tarra* day one foreign frien'   *the other*
> Come spen some time wid mi.
>
> Yuh have no freedom *fi* go up and down   *to*
> unless yuh have *smaddy*   *somebody*
> *fi keep dat pickney deh.*   *to look after that child*

Writers such as the Jamaican James Berry use a language which can be described as a mixture of Standard English and creole, or **modified creole**:

> *I not forgetting* that dressing up is a Sunday main feature ...
> Me and my big brother walk to church and *no need saying we in* our best clothes.

What is a text?

57

> A **text** is a continuous piece of spoken or written
> language, usually with a recognisable start and end
> point.

A text can be defined according to its **purpose**; for example,
to persuade, to inform or to analyse.

Texts which share a common purpose are sometimes known as
text-types. They tend to have particular language features in
common. For example, texts whose purpose is to advise tend
to use a significant number of imperative [imp] and
conditional [c] constructions, as in the quotes from the police
advice brochure, below:

> Only *use* [imp] a reputable taxi company. *Ask* [imp] around
> your friends *if you don't know one* [c].
>
> *If you are being picked up by a Private Hire vehicle* [c],
> *ask* [imp] the driver who he is there to collect.
>
> *Remember!* [imp]
>
> *Don't* [imp] jump in the first car that pulls up.
>
> *If you are unhappy with the conduct of the driver* [c], *make* [imp]
> a note of the licence plate number.

imperative mood >>> pages 78–9

conditional clauses >>> page 73

For some linguists, a text is no different from a **discourse**, the term given to any connected piece of speech or writing longer than a conventional sentence. Other linguists argue that a text has to have a start and an end point. Some use 'text' for writing and 'discourse' for speech.

Genre

58

> A **genre** is a particular kind of text with its own readily identifiable distinguishing features which have remained stable over a period of time.

The features which identify a genre can include story elements, structure, and language patterns.

For example, a typical folk tale might include the following:
- story elements:

  a task or puzzle, a poor but honest hero or heroine, magic spells

- structure:

  things happening in threes, a secret revealed at the end

- language patterns:

  Once upon a time... And they lived happily ever after.

 ## Sub-genres

Familiar genres in the western world include: poetry, the folk tale, autobiography...

But many of these can also be divided into sub-genres. For example, prose fiction might be sub-divided according to **form** into *the novel, the short story, the novella, the mini-saga...* It might also be sub-divided according to **categories**, such as:

- fantasy:

> One Ring to rule them all, One Ring to find them
> One Ring to bring them all and in the darkness bind
> them.

- the supernatural:

> 'The spectre came back a week ago. Ever since, it has been
> there, now and again, by fits and starts.'

- horror:

> Laughter, a high-pitched, frightening laughter shook her as
> she looked at the red naked footprints which led away
> from the bedside, across the floor and down the stairs, after
> the doctor...

- comedy:

> He took pen and some paper. 'Now. Name of elephant?'
> 'Hassan Ben Ali Ben Selim Abdallah Mohammed Moisé
> Alhammal Jamsetjejeebhoy Dhuleep Sultan Ebu Bhudpoor.'
> 'Very well. Given name?'
> 'Jumbo.'

- detective story:

> 'This affair must all be unravelled from within.' He tapped
> his forehead. 'These little grey cells. It is "up to them" – as
> you say over here.'

Many texts will be of mixed genre – such as historical detective story – while a single magazine or website will contain examples of numerous different genres and sub-genres: interviews, recipes, brief 'biogs'...

Parody

> A **parody** is a comic text which mocks and subverts a particular genre, style or author, through imitation and/or exaggeration.

- Some parodies are close imitations of particular writers or even single works. For example, John Masefield's 'Sea Fever' famously begins:

> I must down to the seas again, to the lonely sea and the sky
> And all I ask is a tall ship and a star to steer her by

Spike Milligan parodied it as:

> I must go down to the sea again, the lonely sea and the sky
> I left my pants and socks there – I wonder if they're dry?

- Other parodies mock a whole genre. This is from *Red Dwarf*, a parody of science fiction films:

CAT: Well, what are we waiting for?
RIMMER: Without deflectors? What about Space Corps
              Directive one-seven-four-two?
KRYTEN: One-seven-four-two? 'No member of the Corps
              should ever report for active duty in a ginger
              toupee'?

Audience

> Audience is the name given to the people who are
> expected to read or see a text – the group to whom
> that text is addressed.

The term can refer to any readers, listeners, film and television
audiences or users of information technology.

An audience for a text can be, for example:

- very wide, e.g. all teenagers, all gardeners, everybody who
  watches television, readers of fiction:

> ### EastEnders (8pm)
>
> Mark (Todd Carty) and Lisa (Lucy
> Benjamin) move in with Pauline (Wendy
> Richard)…

- a group, e.g. members of a local sports club, your
  neighbours, a particular interest group:

> The suggestion that the council
> should install traffic-calming
> measures in Holloway Road has had
> a mixed response...

- a particular individual, e.g. a friend or relative, the secretary of a company, a newspaper editor:

> *...From my doleful prison on the Tower, this sixth of May.*
> *Your most loyal and ever faithful wife,*
> *Anne Boleyn*

- yourself, e.g. in a diary or journal, a shopping list or a note to remind yourself to do something:

> **Saturday**
>
> *Saturday morning; arriving at Glastonbury it's rain, rain, rain...*

Register

61

> Register is the term given to the style of language we choose, to suit a particular audience, situation, social context and subject-matter.

Formal and informal registers

The most obvious distinction in registers is between:

- **formal register** used in more formal contexts, and
- **informal register** used between friends or in more relaxed situations. Informal register can include:

colloquial language >>> pages 136–7

slang >>> pages 138–9

jargon >>> page 135

regional dialect >>> pages 120–1

Common and specialist registers

We might also distinguish between the **common register**, which we all use, and the more **specialist registers** employed in a variety of particular contexts.

Common register

An example of the common register is this extract by George Orwell. It does not contain any language which would limit its relevance to a particular audience or context:

> From a very early age, perhaps the age of five or six, I knew that when I grew up I should be a writer. Between the ages of about seventeen and twenty-four I tried to abandon the idea...

Specialist registers are aimed at particular audiences and used in particular contexts. Two of the most easily identified are the scientific register and the technical register.

The scientific register

David Attenborough's description of the Venus fly-trap is an example of the scientific register, with its factual content and specialist biological terms:

> It too is a rosette a few inches across. It has narrow green leaves that at the end are prolonged into two reddish, kidney-shaped lobes on either side of the midrib.

The technical register

This example of the technical register is taken from a Macintosh user's manual. It assumes that the reader understands the specialist terms and it has a specific, limited use:

> This icon usually means that the computer can't find system software on the hard disk or any disks attached to the computer. You may need to reinstall system software.

Scientific and technical registers often include **jargon**: the set of words and expressions peculiar to a particular trade, profession or activity:

> In the second *set* Henman twice *double-faulted* at *deuce*...

For people who understand a particular jargon, it is a useful and exact shorthand. But it can be irritating when its purpose is simply to make an ordinary statement seem grand:

Colloquial language

62

> Colloquial language is used in informal situations.

The term usually applies to speech; but **colloquialisms** can also be found in certain kinds of writing.

Colloquial language will often contain:
- contractions, e.g. *I've, you're, she's…*
- connecting words and phrases, e.g. *you know*
- tag questions, e.g. *isn't it? didn't we?*
- minor sentences, e.g. *Right. No problem. Done!*
- slang words and expressions

slang >>> pages 138–9

Articles in tabloid newspapers are often written in a colloquial style. Examples have been highlighted in this extract from the *Sun*:

Punter **Adrian Fitzpatrick** *pocketed* **£11,700 – thanks to an amazing soccer** *punch-up*.

THE MILLIONAIRE FLORIST bet that Celtic, Brighton and Sheffield United would all win on Saturday.

The first two *came up trumps*, but Adrian's bid for a £30,712 win *went pear-shaped* as United went down 3-0.

His bet *looked sunk* – until three minutes from time.

Appropriate v. correct

We all use colloquial language in speech, and often, for example, when writing informal, personal letters. In those contexts we would say that colloquial language was 'appropriate' (rather than 'correct'). We would also agree that it was usually inappropriate in formal writing, such as business letters or scientific papers.

The preference for the notion of appropriateness rather than correctness is part of a **descriptive** approach to language, which takes the view that language is:
- ever-changing, rather than fixed
- varied, rather than uniform

In a descriptive approach we would attempt to describe and explain the differences between colloquial and formal language without suggesting that one was 'better' than the other.

Older grammars often adopted a **prescriptive** approach, based on the opinion that some forms of language have a higher value than others and ought to be aspired to at all times. This approach is often linked to a **proscriptive** one, in which rules are formulated to tell language users what they may *not* do.

Slang

63

> Slang is a set of words and expressions heard in colloquial language, often used to add vividness or humour.

- While many colloquialisms are familiar and comfortable, because they have been around for a long time, slang expressions are consciously colourful and can have a mild shock value. In certain contexts their use can even be anarchic:

  It is about time we pulled our fingers out!
  (Prince Philip, talking about British industry in 1961)

- Slang expressions are often created by giving a familiar concept an imaginative metaphorical twist. However, expressions such as *he's one sandwich short of a picnic* often become clichés.

cliché >>> pages 142–3

- Most examples of slang are ephemeral and date very quickly. For example, no-one these days would say:

  Oh, but good lord! That must have been *simply topping*!
  (1928)

  And the same would apply to other slang terms for excellence, such as *fab* and *gear* (early 1960s) or *awesome* (1980s) – though *cool* (1940s) made an unexpected return in the 1990s.

- It is often difficult to distinguish between slang and colloquialism. Sometimes a slang expression will even come to be used in formal contexts (as has happened with *mob* and *blurb*, for example).
- Slang is usually developed by a particular group, but will often gain a wider currency in colloquial language. When that happens it tends to lose its edge. For example, the expression 'take the micky' is popularly heard in polite circles. Few users are aware that it derives from cockney rhyming slang 'take the Micky Bliss'.

Idiom

64

> An **idiom** is an expression which cannot be understood simply by considering its constituent parts.

Another way of looking at it is to say that an idiom is unique to a particular language. For example, a foreign language speaker would not understand an expression such as *Shakespeare kicked the bucket in 1616* if they were to hear a word-for-word translation.

Common **idiomatic expressions** in English include:

You've got to hand it to her
They were born on foreign soil
That's only the tip of the iceberg
We're going to have to stick to our guns
He let the cat out of the bag

- Most idioms are fixed. You cannot, for example, say: *the bucket was kicked by Shakespeare* without the expression losing its idiomatic meaning. Nor could you say *he kicked the pail* or *he side-footed the bucket* or *he went in for some bucket-kicking* (unless you were engaging in conscious wordplay).
- There are some exceptions. For example, with an idiom like *let the cat out of the bag*, it is possible to say: *The cat has been well and truly let out of the bag this time.*

Cliché

65

> A cliché is a word or phrase that has lost its
> freshness through over-use.

Many clichés tend to be:

- idioms and stock expressions (all of the following from one
  tennis article in the *Guardian*):

> to go off the rails, let's face it, the jury's still out on that
> one, a totally different ball-game, put their foot in it

idiom >>> pages 140–1

- proverbial expressions:

> don't count your chickens, no stone left unturned,
> wouldn't say 'boo' to a goose

- similes:

> as dead as a doornail, spread like wildfire, like a bull in a
> china-shop, as mad as a hatter, strong as an ox

Webster's Dictionary of English Usage has suggested two
approaches which can help to identify a cliché:

'*You might ... want to base your notion of a cliché not on the
expression itself but on its use; if it seems to be used without much
reference to a definite meaning, it is then perhaps a cliché.
... A second and more workable approach might be to call a cliché
whatever word or expression you have heard or seen often enough to
find annoying.*'

- The term *cliché* can also apply to any over-used formula in, for example, cinema or music.
- All clichés must at some time have been fresh and original expressions: there must have been a first time a disappointed footballer was 'sick as a parrot'.

Metaphor and simile

66

> **Figurative language** is characterised by its use of figures of speech: devices that achieve special effects by using words in distinctive ways.

Among the most widely used figures of speech are **metaphor** and **simile**.

> A **metaphor** is a figure of speech involving comparison in which the user describes one thing or action as though it were something else.

Metaphors are common in literature:

> I saw we moved together.
> Often we were a bike, ridden
> on two flat tyres.
> My mind, dear wife, is full of scorpions

and in everyday speech:

> her face *lit up*
>
> they *flocked* to see it
>
> we've got to *take steps* to put this right
>
> Chaucer is the *father* of modern poetry
>
> I can't *stand* it

Metaphors like these, which have become so much a part of everyday language that they are no longer thought of as metaphorical, are known as **dead metaphors**.

> A **simile** is a figure of speech in which things are compared in an unusual or unexpected way, using *like* or *as*.

Like metaphors, similes are widely used in literature:

Your face, my thane, is as a book where men may read strange matters

...her hair stood out from her head like a crest of serpents

and in everyday language:

these will sell like hot cakes

he was like a fish out of water

Two figures of speech closely related to metaphor are personification and metonymy.

- **Personification** is a kind of metaphor in which animals, inanimate objects, the elements and ideas are given human attributes:

Life was always playing dirty tricks on her.

- In **metonymy** something is labelled by the name of something associated with it. We commonly refer to the monarchy as 'the Crown', for example, or say that someone is addicted to 'the bottle'.

Effects and meanings 67

> **Lexical figures of speech** depend for their effect upon meaning.
>
> **Phonological figures of speech** depend upon the sounds of words.

Metaphor, simile, personification and metonymy are examples of lexical figures of speech. Others include: *bathos, hyperbole, paradox, oxymoron, euphemism* and *irony*.

- **Bathos** is the conscious use of anticlimax:

  'Hear me! Hear me!' thundered Big Beard… 'Britain has hundreds and hundreds of miles of canals! Dug with sweat and blood and… and… shovels,' he continued, slipping from his oratory peak for a moment.

- **Hyperbole** is conscious exaggeration or overstatement, usually not to be taken literally:

  'Look at the table… knee-deep in scorpions… Every matchbox in this house is a deathtrap'

- A **paradox** is a statement which seems contradictory but contains an insight:

  The Child is father of the Man.

  It was the best of times, it was the worst of times.

  Nowadays people know the price of everything and the value of nothing.

- In **oxymoron**, opposites are brought together in an apparent paradox:

  Parting is such sweet sorrow

  I must be cruel only to be kind

- **Euphemism** is the use of a mild or evasive expression to replace one that is taboo, offensive, or has unpleasant connotations:

  'Well, you want to tell whoever saw me to mind their own *fizzing* business.'

Irony

> Irony is the use of words to imply something
> opposite to their surface meaning.

In this example, a seemingly complacent tone is used by Great
War poet Siegfried Sassoon to convey anger and bitterness:

> Does it matter? – losing your legs?…
> For people will always be kind
> And you need not show that you mind
> When the others come in after hunting
> To gobble their muffins and eggs.

- In **dramatic irony**, the audience knows something that
  the character does not. For example, when King Duncan
  rues the treachery of Cawdor with the observation that:
  'He was a gentleman on whom I built
  An absolute trust –',
  there is dramatic irony when Macbeth (who the audience
  know is plotting to murder Duncan) not only enters at
  that very moment, but is greeted with:
  'O worthiest cousin!'
- Whereas irony usually works through pretence and
  implication, **sarcasm** attacks openly. For example, if a
  driving-instructor crashed the car, the learner sitting
  next to him might observe:

  That was an interesting three-point turn.   **irony**

  or

  You really are a brilliant teacher, aren't you!   **sarcasm**

  Sarcasm is often conveyed by tone of voice.

> Phonological figures of speech achieve their effects through sound.

They include alliteration and onomatopoeia.

- **Alliteration** is the repetition of sounds, usually initial consonant sounds. It is especially common in:
  - advertising:

    Pick up a Penguin

    You can be sure of Shell

    Put a tiger in your tank

  - certain forms of storytelling:

    ...the great grey-green greasy Limpopo River

  - newspaper headlines:

    It's gloomy for Goram

    Happy Hammer Paolo

- **Onomatopoeia** is the use of sounds to echo meaning. It is common in daily language:

  click, snap, thump, cuckoo, tick-tock

  and widely used in poetry:

  Only the *stuttering* rifles' rapid rattle
  Can *patter* out their hasty orisons

Words, sounds and meanings

70

Linguists sometimes describe words in terms of **phonemes**, **morphemes**, **lexemes** and **graphemes**. The suffix *-eme* means 'a unit of language'.

> **A phoneme is the basic unit of *sound* in a word.**

For example, *cat* is made up of three phonemes: the initial consonant sound, the medial vowel sound, and the final consonant sound.

A phoneme can be represented in writing by one, two, three or four letters. For example, in Received Pronunciation, the following groups of words all end in the same phoneme:

to, y**ou**, sh**oe**, thr**ough**
sh**e**, b**ee**, L**eigh** on S**ea**

Received Pronunciation >>> page 119

- **Phonetics** is the scientific study of speech sounds; **phonology**, a branch of linguistics, is concerned with the principles that govern the *patterns* of sound in a language.
- Phonologists are also interested in **prosody** – stress, rhythm and intonation of everyday speech.

> **A morpheme is the smallest unit of *meaning* in a word.**

A morpheme can be as long as the word *elephant*, or as short as the *s* which marks the plural in *elephants*.

For example:
> *hand* is made up of one morpheme
> *hand* / *s* of two morphemes
> *hand* / *writ* / *ing* of three morphemes

A single morpheme can be pronounced in different ways. For example, in RP, the past tense morpheme *ed* is pronounced:

> /**d**/ in *hurled*, /**id**/ in *spotted*, and /**t**/ in *talked*

> **A lexeme is a unit of *vocabulary*.**

A lexeme can be represented by:
- a single word, e.g. *banana, puce, oscillate*
- two or more words which make up a single unit of meaning, e.g. *shut up, come in, sit down*
- an idiomatic expression, e.g. *round the bend, over the moon, putting all [his] eggs in one basket*

idiom >>> pages 140–1

> **A grapheme** is the basic unit of *writing* and represents a single phoneme.

A single phoneme can be represented by a range of different graphemes. This happens, for example, with the phoneme /**s**/ in the following words:

bit**s**, mou**s**e, mi**ce**, **c**ity, **sc**ien**ce**, **ps**ychology

- A grapheme in a particular word can represent a variety of different phonemes. For example, the grapheme *a* in *bath* will not represent the same phoneme for both Londoners and Mancunians.

- A group of letters which represents a phoneme or morpheme is sometimes called a **letter string**.

Roots

> The terms **root** and **affix** are used to describe the way in which words are formed. The root is the basic structural element of a word. An affix is a morpheme which can be attached to a root. Affixes can be prefixes or suffixes.

prefixes >>> pages 154–5

suffixes >>> pages 156–7

For example, the affixes *un–*, *-ful* and *-ly* can all be added to the root *help* to form *helpful, unhelpful* and *unhelpfully*.

A root does not have to be a complete word. For example, the root in the word *descend* is *–scend*. Affixes could be added to it, to form, for example: *ascends, descending* or *ascendant*.

- A root is different from a **root word**. A root word is the 'ancestor' of a modern word. For example, the Latin *femina* (a woman) is the root word from which we get *feminine*.
- A **base** is a word or word element from which another is derived. For example, the base of *sharpen* is *sharp*; the base of *sharpener* is *sharpen*.

Prefixes

> A **prefix** is an affix added at the beginning of a root or base, to form a new word.

affix, root, base >>> page 153

For example:

prefix	root
un-	*kind*
co-	*habit*
multi-	*purpose*
non-	*metallic*
re-	*usable*

● All prefixes are **lexical** – that is to say, they affect *meaning*. For example, **negative prefixes**, as their name suggests, create a negative meaning:

likely – *un*likely
religious – *ir*religious
moral – *a*moral

- Numerical prefixes are widely used in fields such as mathematics and music:

*semi*quaver, *bi*sect, *dodeca*hedron, *kilo*metre

but not exclusively:

'It is not necessary that every time he rises he should give his imitation of a *semi*-house-trained polecat.'

- Sometimes two prefixes can be used together:

un- re- pentant
anti- dis- establishment
ir- re- placeable

occasionally more than two:

hemi- demi- semi- quaver

prefixes and their meanings >>> pages 166–7

Suffixes

73

> A **suffix** is an affix added at the end of a root or base, to form a new word.

affix, root, base >>> page 153

There are two kinds of suffix:
- inflectional suffixes
- derivational suffixes

Inflectional suffixes

Inflectional suffixes are grammatical: they show how a word is being used in the sentence. For example:
- the verb *kick* can be inflected to show:

person	we *kick* (first person)	she *kicks* (third person)
tense	they *kick* (present)	they *kicked* (past)

and to form the **participle** *kicking*

participles >>> pages 58–61

- the noun *traveller* can be inflected to show:

number	one *traveller* (singular)	two *travellers* (plural)
possession	a *traveller's* tale	*travellers'* tales

apostrophe to show possession >>> pages 104–5

- the adjective *thick* can be inflected to show:

comparative	*thicker*
superlative	*thickest*

All of these endings are inflectional suffixes.

Derivational suffixes

Derivational suffixes are lexical, like prefixes: they affect meaning. Examples are:

> dark*ness*, head*ship*, like*able*

Derivational suffixes are used in the formation of:
- verbs, e.g. *advertise*, *lengthen*, *beautify*
- abstract nouns, e.g. *shortage*, *kingdom*, *racism*, *education*, *contentment*
- concrete nouns, e.g. *actress*, *mountaineer*, *weakling*, *informant*
- adverbs, e.g. *clockwise*, *promptly*, *backwards*
- adjectives, e.g. *hairy*, *explosive*, *changeable*

suffixes and their meanings >>> pages 168–70

Forming new words

74

New words are formed in a variety of ways.

> **A compound word is a word made up of two or more existing words.**

Common examples are:

football, handwriting, teapot, blackbird

and, more recently:

cashpoint, postcode, jobshare

These come from everyday language and are therefore known as **vernacular compounds**.

English also contains a large number of **classical compounds**, formed from Latin and ancient Greek:

agrichemicals, geology, autobiography, psychometric

Some compounds are a mixture of vernacular and classical:

biopic, psychobabble, telemarketing

It is difficult to know how to write compound words. Some grammarians distinguish between:
- **solid compounds**, such as *armchair* and *blackberry*, written as one word
- **hyphenated compounds**, such as *road-sweeper* and *many-sided*, written with a hyphen
- **open compounds**, such as *bank clerk* and *railway station*, written as two words

> **A blend is a word formed by fusing together elements of two other existing words.**

Blends are traditionally called **portmanteau words** (after the bag with two compartments).

The most famous example and definition can be found in Lewis Carroll's *Through the Looking Glass*. After reciting a poem which begins:

> 'Twas brillig and the slithy toves
> Did gyre and gimble in the wabe...

Humpty Dumpty explains:

> 'Well, "*slithy*" means "lithe and slimy" ... You see it's like a portmanteau — there are two meanings packed up into one word.'

More recent examples are:

smog	from *smoke* and *fog*
brunch	from *breakfast* and *lunch*
electrocute	from *electric* and *execute*
Oxbridge	from *Oxford* and *Cambridge*
readathon	from *read* and *marathon*
motorcade	from *motor* and *cavalcade*
motel	from *motor* and *hotel*
vegeburger	from *vegetarian* and *hamburger*

> **Conversion is the term given to the use of one word-class with the function of the other.**

This happens most commonly with nouns used as verbs. For example, the noun *access* has in recent years been widely used as a verb:

> You can *access* it on the website.

> **A coinage** is a new word or phrase – or an old one used in a new sense.

Newly created words and phrases are also sometimes called **neologisms**. Neologisms arise most commonly through:

- compounding:

  couch potato (first recorded in 1976), *Ceefax* (early 1970s), *Euro-sceptic* (1980s)

- derivation:

  yuppie (from young urban – or upwardly mobile – professional, mid–1980s), *PIN* (personal identification number, mid–1980s)

- adopting a new meaning:

  icon (early 1980s), *spin-doctor* (someone who presents political stories in a favourable way – 1984), *doughnutting* (the clustering of MPs around a speaker when a House of Commons debate is televised, to make it look as though the House is full – 1989)

- borrowing:

  nouvelle cuisine (late 1970s), *glasnost* (a policy of freedom of information in the Soviet Union – 1985), *fatwa* (a legal ruling given by an Islamic religious leader – 1989)

Abbreviations can also be a rich source of neologisms, especially when they are acronyms.

> An **acronym** is an abbreviation made up of the initial letters of a series of words and pronounced as a single word.

Many acronyms are part of our day–to–day language:

radar *(radio detection and ranging)*

laser *(light amplification by the stimulated emission of radiation)*

RAM *(random access memory)*

Aids *(acquired immune deficiency syndrome)*

NATO *(North Atlantic Treaty Organisation)*

UNESCO *(United Nations Educational, Scientific, and Cultural Organisation)*

SALT *(Strategic Arms Limitation Talks)*

CERN *(Centre Européen pour la recherche nucléaire)*

Neologisms cease to be neologisms once they have been in common use for a while, as the following examples – and many on the previous page – show:

apartheid, crash landing, genocide (1940s)

fast-food, sitcom, theme park (1960s)

cashpoint, golden handshake, silent majority (1980s)

Synonyms and antonyms

75

> Synonyms are words which share the same meaning.

We often use synonyms to elucidate our meaning. For example:

> '...I will be frank with you.'
> 'I beg your pardon – will be what?'
> '*Frank – open –* perfectly *candid.*'

This next speech depends for its effect upon our knowledge of synonymous idiomatic expressions for *dead*:

> It's not pining – it's *passed on*! This parrot is *no more*! It *has ceased to be*! It's *expired* and *gone to meet its maker*! This is a *late* parrot! It's *a stiff*! *Bereft of life it rests in peace* – if you hadn't nailed it to the perch it would be *pushing up the daisies*! It's *rung down the curtain* and *joined the choir invisible*! THIS IS AN EX-PARROT!

idiom >>> pages 140–1

> Many linguists argue that there is no such thing as a synonym, because no two words have exactly the same **connotations** or are used in the same **context**.

> **A word which has an opposite meaning to another is called an antonym.**

An antonym can be 'opposite' in three different ways:

- **gradable** antonyms include:

  hot – cold,   high – low,   fast – slow,   wet – dry,
  happy – sad

  Gradable antonyms can be put on a graded scale (e.g. with *very hot* at one end and *very cold* at the other):

  You ought to get out of those wet clothes and into a dry Martini.

- **complementary** antonyms include:

  male – female,   dead – alive,   single – married

  These express an either/or relationship: you are either *dead* or *alive*:

  God is not dead but alive and well and working on a much less ambitious project.

- **converse** antonyms include:

  buy – sell,   borrow – lend,   wife – husband

  These are dependent on one another: you can't *buy* without someone *selling*.

  This line from *The Merchant of Venice* contains both gradable antonyms (*light – heavy*) and converse antonyms (*wife – husband*):

  For a light wife doth make a heavy husband.

> Some words have different antonyms in different contexts. For example, the antonym of *light* can be either *heavy* or *dark*.

Homonyms

76

> **Homonyms are words which are identical in spelling and/or pronunciation, but different in meaning and/or origin.**

There are three kinds of homonym:

- Some **homographs** are identical in spelling and pronunciation, but different in meaning and origin. Examples include the word *flag*:

  1 (noun) a kind of plant growing on moist ground
  2 (noun and verb) flat slab of rock for paving
  3 (noun) quill-feather of bird's wing
  4 (noun and verb) piece of bunting attached to a staff
  5 (verb) droop, fade, become limp

- Other **homographs** are identical in spelling but different in meaning, origin *and pronunciation*. For example:

  I *refuse* to look after your *refuse*.

  Lead me to some *lead* piping.

  As the speeches increased in *number*, my aching bottom became *number*.

  Other examples include:

  incense, entrance, minute, supply, bow, wind

- **Homophones** are words which are identical in pronunciation but different in spelling and meaning. Examples of homophones in RP are: *course/coarse*, *led/lead*, *dye/die*, *beer/bier*, *there/their/they're*, *I'll/aisle*, *reed/read*, *pair/pear* and *right/write/rite*.

Homophones can form the basis of some effective wordplay:

> His death, which happened in his *berth*,
> At forty-odd befell:
> They went and *told* the sexton and
> The sexton *toll'd* the bell.

Words can be homophones in one variety of English but not in another. For example, the following pairs of words are all homophones in RP, but not in Scottish accents:

turn / tern
weather / whether
father / farther

Common prefixes and their meanings

Prefix	Meaning	Example
a	negation	amoral
ab	from	absence
ad	towards	advance
amb/amph	on both sides	ambidextrous
ante	before	ante-room
anti	against	antiseptic
aqu	water	aqueduct
arch	chief	archbishop
aud/aur	hearing	audible
auto	self	autobiography
ben	well	beneficent
bi	two	binoculars
bio	life	biography
cent	hundred	century
co	together	cohabit
contra	against	contraflow
counter	opposite	counter-clockwise
cycl	circle/around	cyclone
de	reversal	defrost
demi	half	demi-god
di	two	digraph
dis	negation	disappear
dis	reversal	disconnect
ex	out of / former	expel/ex-partner
extra	outside/beyond	extraordinary
fore	in front of	foreground
geo	Earth	geography
hemi	half	hemisphere
hydro	water	hydro-electric
hyper	over and above	hypertext
in	negation	intolerant
inter	between	interview
intra	inside	intravenous
kilo	thousand	kilogram
mal	badly	malfunction
mega	great	megalith

meta	with/change	metalanguage/ metamorphic
micro/mini	small	microcosm/minibus
milli	thousand	millipede
mono	one	monorail
multi	many	multiply
neo	new	neo-classical
non	negation	non-smoker
omni	all	omnivorous
opti	seeing	optical
paleo	old	paleolithic
pan	all	pan-African
phono	sound	phonology
photo	light	photography
poly	many	polygon
post	after	postwar
pre	before	predict
pro	for	Pro-European
proto	first, original	proto-type
pseud	false	pseudonym
psych	the mind	psychiatrist
re	again	review
retro	back again	retrograde
semi	half	semicircle
sub	under	submarine
super/sur	above	supersonic/surtax
tele	at a distance	telescope
terr	land	territorial
theo	god	theology
trans	across	transatlantic
tri	three	tricycle
ultra	beyond	ultramodern
un	negation	unwise
un	reversal	undo
uni	one	unicycle
vice	substitute	vice-captain
zoo	animals	zoology

Common suffixes and their meanings

Suffix	Forms: n/v/adj/ adv	Meaning	Example
-able/-ible/ -ble/-uble	adj		readable, legible
-age	n		mileage
-al	n		refusal
-an/-ian/ -arian	n/adj	membership	Roman/Parisian/ vegetarian
-ant	n	person	informant
-arch/-archy	n	ruler	monarch, monarchy
-ary	n/adj		dictionary/contrary
-ate	1 adj		passionate
	2 n	status	magistrate
	3 v		dominate
-ation	n		creation
-cide	n	killing	suicide
-cracy/-crat	n	government	democracy/democrat
-cule/-cle	n	diminutive	molecule/particle
-cy	n	state of being	infancy
-dom	n	condition	freedom
-ed	v/adj		kicked/pointed
-ee	n	person	employee
-en	v		deafen
-er	adj	comparative	larger
-er/-or/-eer	n	doer	employer/doctor/ mountaineer
-ery	n	condition	slavery
-ese	n/adj	person	Chinese
-esque	adj	in the style of	Pinteresque
-ess	n	feminine	tigress
-est/-iest	adj	superlative	largest/funniest
-ette	n	diminutive	kitchenette
-faction	n		satisfaction
-ferous/ -iferous	adj	carrying	fossiliferous
-fold	adj/adv	multiplied by	twofold

-ful	1 adj	full of	truthful
	2 n	amount	handful
-fy	v	make	purify
-gen	n	producing	oxygen
-gon	n	having angles	polygon
-gram/ -graph/ -graphy	n	written/ drawn	diagram/photograph/ geography
-hood	n	condition	childhood
-ic/-ical	1 adj		comic/comical
	2 n	arts	music/musical
-ician	n	skilled person	musician
-icity	n		publicity
-ification	n	action	purification
-ing	n/adj		reading
-ion/-sion/ -tion/-xion	n	condition/ action	dominion/dimension/ attraction/ crucifixion
-ise/-ize	v		realise/civilize
-ish	1 adj	'sort of'	bluish
	2 adj	nationality	Swedish
-ism	n		criticism
-ist	n	doer/supporter	cyclist/socialist
-ite	1 n	mineral	kryptonite
	2 n	follower	Luddite
-itis	n	inflammation	tonsilitis
-ive	adj		active
-kin	n	diminutive	lambkin
-less	adj	without/ unable	hopeless/countless
-ling	n	diminutive/ with a quality	duckling/weakling
-logy/ -logist	n/adj n	study/ expert	biology/ biologist
-ly	1 adj		friendly
	2 adv		stupidly
-meter	n	measuring	barometer
-most	adj	superlative	uppermost
-ness	n	condition	kindness
-oid	n/adj	shape	spheroid

–ous	adj		desirous
–pathy	n	feeling	sympathy
–phobia	n	fear/dislike	claustrophobia
–phone/ –phonic	n/adj	hearing	telephone/ polyphonic
–scope/ –scopic	n/adj	seeing	telescope/ microscopic
–ship	n	condition	friendship
–some	adj	quality	quarrelsome
–ster	n	doer	gangster
–teen	n		fourteen
–tude	n	condition	solitude
–vore/ –vorous	n/adj	eating	carnivore/ carnivorous
–ward/ –wards	adj/adv	direction	homeward/ backwards
–ways	adv	manner	sideways
–wise	adv	manner	clockwise
–y/–ie	n	diminutive	aunty/Annie

List of quotations

from fiction, poetry, drama and speeches

(Details have not been given for newspaper articles, film or song titles or well-known expressions.)

Section	Quotation	Author	Work
1	*One evening...*	Thomas Hardy	*The Mayor of Casterbridge*
	To walk...?	A Conan Doyle	*The Hound of the Baskervilles*
	But what...?	Charles Dickens	*A Christmas Carol*
	And when...	Jane Austen	*Pride and Prejudice*
2	*The patient...*	Charles Dickens	*Oliver Twist*
	Morgan found...	RL Stevenson	*Treasure Island*
	I have...	Martin Luther King	speech of 28 August 1963
3	*Virginia blushed...* [etc]	Oscar Wilde	*The Canterville Ghost*
4	*The wife...* [etc]	Jonathan Swift	*Gulliver's Travels*
	they never... [etc]	JRR Tolkien	*The Hobbit*
5	*I sipped...*	Bill Bryson	*Notes from a Small Island*
	Reader, I...	Charlotte Brontë	*Jane Eyre*
	I can...	Peter Shaffer	*Amadeus*
	You never...	Harold Pinter	*The Dumb Waiter*
	Will you...? [etc]	PG Wodehouse	*The Mating Season*
	I had eggs...	Bill Bryson	*Notes from a Small Island*
6	*You are...*	William Shakespeare	*Othello*
	I grow...	TS Eliot	*The Love Song of J Alfred Prufrock*
	I am...	William Shakespeare	*Hamlet*
	This fellow's...	William Shakespeare	*Twelfth Night*
	Are not...?	William Shakespeare	*A Midsummer Night's Dream*

	THAT'S HIM!	Robert Browning	*The Jackdaw of Rheims*
	No, that's...	PG Wodehouse	*The Mating Season*
	We consider...	Abraham Lincoln	speech of 8 September 1858
7	*Frankly, my...*	Margaret Mitchell	*Gone With the Wind*
	Marry, sir...	William Shakespeare	*Much Ado About Nothing*
	'Nephew!' returned... [etc]	Charles Dickens	*A Christmas Carol*
8	*My father...*	Jonathan Swift	*Gulliver's Travels*
	In a hole...	JRR Tolkien	*The Hobbit*
	In Troy...	William Shakespeare	*Troilus and Cressida*
	But what...?	RL Stevenson	*Treasure Island*
	Are you...?	Charles Dickens	*A Christmas Carol*
	Who's there?	William Shakespeare	*Hamlet*
	Burn that...	Athol Fugard	*Sizwe Bansi Is Dead*
	And please...	JRR Tolkien	*The Hobbit*
	Bring some...	RC Sherriff	*Journey's End*
	How sweet...	William Shakespeare	*The Merchant of Venice*
	Well, come...	RL Stevenson	*Treasure Island*
	And you're...	JRR Tolkien	*The Hobbit*
	Ever had...? [etc]	RC Sherriff	*Journey's End*
9	*I had...*	RC Sherriff	*Journey's End*
	I exchanged...	Bill Bryson	*Notes from a Small Island*
	...every second...	Harold Pinter	*The Birthday Party*
	In these...	Charles Dickens	*Our Mutual Friend*
	Even the...	Charles Dickens	*A Christmas Carol*
10	*Elizabeth-Jane...*	Thomas Hardy	*The Mayor of Casterbridge*
11	*Far in...*	Charles Dickens	*A Christmas Carol*
12	*Danny...*	Roald Dahl	*Danny, Champion of the World*
	Mr Robert...	Athol Fugard	*Sizwe Bansi Is Dead*

	one can...	George Orwell	*Politics and the English Language*
	A Jug...	Edward Fitzgerald	*The Rubá'iyát of Omar Khayyám, 4.xii*
13	*They could...*	JRR Tolkien	*The Hobbit*
	I feel...	F Scott Fitzgerald	*The Great Gatsby*
	All the people...	Rudyard Kipling	*We and They*
	He built...	F Scott Fitzgerald	*The Great Gatsby*
	I didn't know...	Lewis Carroll	*Alice's Adventures in Wonderland*
	My kingdom...	William Shakespeare	*Richard III*
	Who do...? *then there's...*	Keith Waterhouse	*Billy Liar*
	So long...	William Shakespeare	*Sonnet 18*
	We are responsible...	JB Priestley	*An Inspector Calls*
	something nasty...	Stella Gibbons	*Cold Comfort Farm*
	When everyone is...	WS Gilbert	*The Gondoliers*
	One doesn't like...	PG Wodehouse	*The Mating Season*
	They shut...	Rudyard Kipling	*The Way through the Woods*
	The tree...	Joseph Conrad	*Nostromo*
14	*This...*	David Storey	*This Sporting Life*
	Our...	Thornton Wilder	*Our Town*
	All...	Arthur Miller	*All My Sons*
	What job...?	Keith Waterhouse	*Billy Liar*
	What is...?	WH Davies	*Leisure*
	Yea, twice...	William Shakespeare	*The Merchant of Venice*
	but you cannot...	Abraham Lincoln	speech of 8 September 1858
	The Seven...	TE Lawrence	*The Seven Pillars of Wisdom*
	And all shall...	William Shakespeare	*A Midsummer Night's Dream*

15	*A good, honest...*	Samuel Pepys	*Diary,* 17 March 1661
	I grant him...	William Shakespeare	*Macbeth*
	I could see...	PG Wodehouse	*The Code of the Woosters*
	I'm not the...	Woody Allen	*Sleepers*
	You cannot be...	Logan Pearsall Smith	*Afterthoughts*
	That is why...	Wilfred Owen	*Preface to Poems*
	were it not...	William Shakespeare	*Henry IV, Part One*
	the crown imperial	William Shakespeare	*Henry V*
	The Diamond...	F Scott Fitzgerald	*The Diamond as Big as the Ritz*
	The short...	Thomas Gray	*Elegy ... in a Country Churchyard*
	The poor man...	CF Alexander	*All Things Bright and Beautiful*
16	*the sloeblack...*	Dylan Thomas	*Under Milk Wood*
	At the still...	TS Eliot	*Burnt Norton*
	The man who listens...	GB Shaw	*Man and Superman*
	The Merry...	William Shakespeare	*The Merry Wives of Windsor*
	the moving toyshop...	Alexander Pope	*The Rape of the Lock*
17	*Sir, your...*	William Shakespeare	*Measure for Measure*
	A little...	William Shakespeare	*Hamlet*
	Why, saw...?	William Shakespeare	*Julius Caesar*
	Most wonderful!	William Shakespeare	*Twelfth Night*
	Nothing certainer	William Shakespeare	*Much Ado About Nothing*
	I have learnt...	William Shakespeare	*Macbeth*

How much...	William Shakespeare	*The Merchant of Venice*
This was...	William Shakespeare	*Julius Caesar*
To taste...	William Shakespeare	*The Winter's Tale*
Against the...	William Shakespeare	*Richard II*
tomorrow we...	Dorothy Parker	*Not so deep as a well*
I have dared...	Oscar Wilde	*The Importance of Being Earnest*
To die...	James Barrie	*Peter Pan*
...to speak...	Oscar Wilde	*The Importance of Being Earnest*
I am not quite...	Daisy Ashford	*Young Visitors*
Today we have...	Henry Reed	*Naming of Parts*
They sailed...	Edward Lear	*The Owl and the Pussycat*
The buck...	Harry S Truman	speech of 19 December 1952
I distinctly said...	RC Sherriff	*Journey's End*
Here we go...	TS Eliot	*The Hollow Men*
but for Wales!	Robert Bolt	*A Man For All Seasons*
Now I hold...	Ted Hughes	*Hawk Roosting*
I'll dig...	Seamus Heaney	*Digging*
Oh, in there...!	Kenneth Grahame	*The Wind in the Willows*
Do not fall...	William Shakespeare	*As You Like It*
On Wenlock Edge...	AE Housman	*Wenlock Edge*
Wait till...	Andrew B Sterling	*Wait till the sun shines, Nellie*
while he is near	The Bible	*Isaiah*
Mr Jones...	George Orwell	*Animal Farm*
Jesus wept	The Bible	*The Gospel according to Saint John*
I saw ten...	Bob Dylan	*A Hard Rain's a-Gonna Fall*

The row numbers in the left margin: 18 (tomorrow we...), 19 (Here we go...), 20 (Mr Jones...), 21 (Jesus wept).

	All animals…	George Orwell	*Animal Farm*
	The headmaster said…	Terence Rattigan	*The Browning Version*
	Well, if I…?	James Thurber	cartoon caption: *New Yorker* 5 July 1937
	Because the…	Lennon & McCartney	*Because*
	As Scrooge…	Charles Dickens	*A Christmas Carol*
	It was nearly…	JRR Tolkien	*The Hobbit*
	You know…?	RC Sherriff	*Journey's End*
22	*But surely…?*	Oscar Wilde	*The Importance of Being Earnest*
	a hope that she…	Jane Austen	*Pride and Prejudice*
	I could put…	PG Wodehouse	*Right Ho, Jeeves*
	when they are…	Winston Churchill	speech, 1912
	I have drunk…	William Shakespeare	*The Winter's Tale*
	I've been working…	Lennon & McCartney	*A Hard Day's Night*
	You'll be found…	William Shakespeare	*The Winter's Tale*
	We were put…	Alan Bennett	*Old Country*
	Then you should say…	Lewis Carroll	*Alice's Adventures in Wonderland*
23	*My friend should…*	RL Stevenson	*Treasure Island*
	Will you still…?	Lennon & McCartney	*When I'm Sixty-Four*
	I would…	Andrew Marvell	*To His Coy Mistress*
	He can run…	Joe Louis	*New York Herald Tribune*, 1946
	You could go…	Roald Dahl	*Danny, Champion of the World*
	If I may…	PG Wodehouse	*Right Ho, Jeeves*
	And the hand…	George Eliot	*Silas Marner*
	we must report…	Athol Fugard	*Sizwe Bansi Is Dead*

25	*I'll be revenged...*	William Shakespeare	*Twelfth Night*
	Do I dare...?	TS Eliot	*The Lovesong of J Alfred Prufrock*
	Things we used...	Lennon & McCartney	*Things We Used To Say*
	Am I in...?	GK Chesterton	*Autobiography*
	To sleep...	William Shakespeare	*Hamlet*
26	*the last fading...*	Sir Julian Huxley	*Religion without Revelation*
	And the end...	TS Eliot	*Little Gidding*
	You've missed the...	TS Eliot	*The Cocktail Party*
	No Englishman...	GB Shaw	*Saint Joan*
	The wounded surgeon...	TS Eliot	*East Coker*
	When you're wounded...	Rudyard Kipling	*The Young British Soldier*
	Which will be...	William McGonagall	*The Tay Bridge Disaster*
27	*All animals...*	George Orwell	*Animal Farm*
	I remember...	Laurence Lerner	*I Remember It Well*
	Last week I...	WC Fields	*Godfrey Daniels*
	Either the well...	Lewis Carroll	*Alice's Adventures in Wonderland*
28	*And you can...*	Laurence Lerner	*Nice Work If You Can Get It*
	What happens when...?	Lewis Carroll	*Alice's Adventures in Wonderland*
	I don't know where...	Laurie Lee	*Cider With Rosie*
29	*When you got it...*	Mel Brooks	*The Producers*
	all about the girl...	Lennon & McCartney	*Girl*
	Will you still...	Lennon & McCartney	*When I'm Sixty-Four*

30	*London. Michaelmas...*	Charles Dickens	*Bleak House*
	Oh my!...	Kenneth Grahame	*The Wind in the Willows*
	He did, did he?...	PG Wodehouse	*Right Ho, Jeeves*
31	*I believe you have...*	A Conan Doyle	*The Hound of the Baskervilles*
32	*This is the man, sir...*	William Shakespeare	*Twelfth Night*
33	*As Dad came in... [etc]*	Gene Kemp	*The Turbulent Term of Tyke Tyler*
34	*Harry Potter was... [etc]*	JK Rowling	*Harry Potter and the Prisoner of Azkaban*
36	*oh, I beg... [etc]*	Lewis Carroll	*Alice's Adventures in Wonderland*
	And the pig...	Benjamin Hapgood Burt	*The Pig got up and slowly walked away*
37	*I'm opening out... [etc]*	Lewis Carroll	*Alice's Adventures in Wonderland*
	I have not slept...	Oscar Wilde	*The Canterville Ghost*
	He had hardly...	Charles Dickens	*Barnaby Rudge*
38	*Never use the passive... [etc]*	George Orwell	*Politics and the English Language*
39	*Marley's face.*	Charles Dickens	*A Christmas Carol*
	Squire Trelawney...	RL Stevenson	*Treasure Island*
	Becky, d'you... [etc]	James Berry	*A Thief in the Village*
	Aaaargh! [etc]	Ben Elton	*Gridlock*
40	*I had never... [etc]*	Bill Bryson	*Notes from a Small Island*
	Dear Helene...	Helene Hanff	*84 Charing Cross Road*
41	*They are incapable...*	Tim Haines	*Walking with Dinosaurs*
	Severe pain...	Mike & Tim Birkhead	*The Survival Factor*
	Her matted...	Philip Pullman	*The Amber Spyglass*
	The fine ashes...	McQuire & Kilburn	*Volcanoes of the World*

	On this scale...	Arthur C Clarke	By Space Possessed
42	Her face was...	Philip Pullman	The Amber Spyglass
	Serafina Pekkala...	Philip Pullman	The Subtle Knife
	LISTER...	Grant Naylor	Red Dwarf: Primordial Soup
43	Aisle seven...	Bill Bryson	Notes from a Small Island
	They ordered...	Pamela Stephenson	Billy
	Every occupied...	Jim Parton	Robbie Williams
	When the other...	Tom Baker	Who on Earth is Tom Baker?
	I had a vague...	Bill Bryson	Notes from a Small Island
	KRYTEN...	Grant Naylor	Red Dwarf: Primordial Soup
	he was a relative... and beneath...	Mary Seacole	The Wonderful Adventures of Mary Seacole in Many Lands
	The correct...	Lewis Wolpert	The Unnatural Nature of Science
44	For now I am...	WS Gilbert	Trial by Jury
	Ali...	Alan Garner	The Owl Service
	− Has your mother...?	James Joyce	Portrait of the Artist as a Young Man
	From Lowood...	Charlotte Brontë	Jane Eyre
	I take up...	RL Stevenson	Treasure Island
	D—n Milton!	Henry Fielding	Tom Jones
	Shopping...	Mark Ravenhill	Shopping and F∗∗∗ing
47	My dad'll...	Gene Kemp	The Turbulent Term of Tyke Tyler
48	to-morrow we will...	F Scott Fitzgerald	The Great Gatsby
	His body...	Lindsey Davis	Last Act in Palmyra
	I just wanted...	Ben Elton	Gridlock
49	The Hatter... [etc]	Lewis Carroll	Alice's Adventures in Wonderland

	He exhaled…	Bill Bryson	*Notes from a Small Island*
50	'By "proper treatment"…	PG Wodehouse	*The Code of the Woosters*
	They had titles… [etc]	Bill Bryson	*Notes from a Small Island*
51	'Dick,' said…	RL Stevenson	*Treasure Island*
	'I am… [etc]	Charles Dickens	*A Christmas Carol*
52	Thus, in the midst…	Charles Dickens	*Bleak House*
	How are the mighty…	The Bible	*2 Samuel*
54	Aal except…	Lesley Alexander	*The Magpied Piper of Newcastle on Tyne*
	so we tossed…	Barry Hines	*Kes*
56	Jamaica language…	Valerie Bloom	*Language barrier*
	Yuh have…	Sistren Women's Theatre Group	*Lionheart gal*
	I not forgetting…	James Berry	*A Thief in the Village*
58	One Ring…	JRR Tolkien	*The Lord of the Rings*
	'The spectre…	Charles Dickens	*The Signalman*
	Laughter…	John Wyndham	*Close behind him*
	He took pen…	Mark Twain	*The Stolen White Elephant*
	This affair must…	Agatha Christie	*The Mysterious Affair at Styles*
59	I must down…	John Masefield	*Sea Fever*
	I must go…	Spike Milligan	*Sea Fever*
	Well, what…	Grant Naylor	*Red Dwarf: Primordial Soup*
60	From my doleful…	Anne Boleyn	letter, 1536
	Saturday morning…	Jim Parton	*Robbie Williams*
61	From a very…	George Orwell	*Why I write*
	It too is a rosette…	David Attenborough	*The Trials of Life*
63	Oh, but good lord…!	RC Sherriff	*Journey's End*

66	*I saw we moved...*	James Berry	*A Companionship*
	My mind... *Your face...*	William Shakespeare	*Macbeth*
	her hair...	Philip Pullman	*The Amber Spyglass*
67	*'Hear me!...*	Ben Elton	*Gridlock*
	'Look at...'	Gerald Durrell	*My Family and Other Animals*
	The Child...	William Wordsworth	*My heart leaps up...*
	It was the best...	Charles Dickens	*A Tale of Two Cities*
	Nowadays people...	Oscar Wilde	*Lady Windermere's Fan*
	Parting is...	William Shakespeare	*Romeo and Juliet*
	I must...	William Shakespeare	*Hamlet*
	Well, you want...	Keith Waterhouse	*Billy Liar*
68	*Does it matter?...*	Siegfried Sassoon	*Does it matter?*
69	*the great grey-green...*	Rudyard Kipling	*Just So Stories*
	Only the stuttering...	Wilfred Owen	*Anthem for Doomed Youth*
72	*'It is not necessary...*	Michael Foot [on Norman Tebbit]	speech, 1978
74	*'Twas brillig...* [etc]	Lewis Carroll	*Through the Looking Glass*
75	*'I will be frank...'*	Charles Dickens	*Barnaby Rudge*
	It's not pining...	Graham Chapman et al	*Monty Python's Flying Circus*
	You ought...	Mae West	*Every Day's a Holiday*
	God is not dead...	graffito	*Guardian*, 1975
	For a light...	William Shakespeare	*The Merchant of Venice*
76	*His death...*	Thomas Hood	*Faithless Sally Brown*

Index